Playing with Plays™
Presents
Shakespeare's

Comedy of Errors
FOR KIDS
(The melodramatic version!)

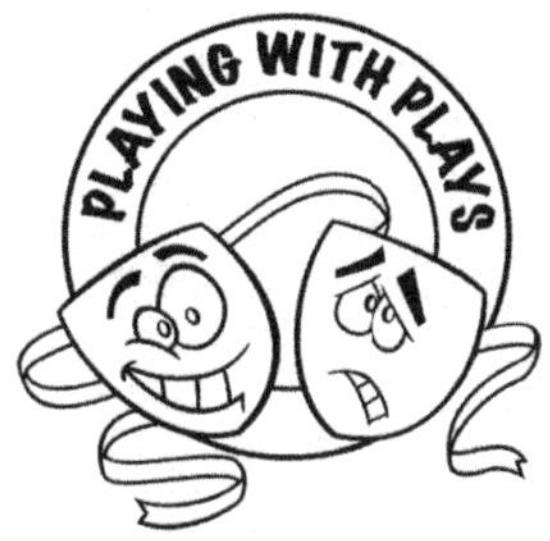

For 9-21+ actors, or kids of all ages who want to have fun!
Creatively modified by
Brendan P. Kelso
Cover Characters by Ron Leishman

3 Melodramatic Modifications of Shakespeare's Play
for 3 different group sizes:

9-12 Actors

11-16+ Actors

14-21+ Actors

Table Of Contents

To all the kids who go over the top
when they're not supposed to.
The kids that push the limits.
The kids that laugh, even at the wrong times.
The kids that ALWAYS have humor in their hearts.
THIS is for you!

-BPK

For performance rights please see page 6 of this book or contact:

contact@PlayingWithPlays.com

Foreword

When I was in high school there was something about Shakespeare that appealed to me. Not that I understood it mind you, but there were clear scenes and images that always stood out in my mind. Romeo & Juliet, "Romeo, Romeo; wherefore art thou Romeo?"; Julius Caesar, "Et tu Brute"; Macbeth, "Double, Double, toil and trouble"; Hamlet, "to be or not to be"; A Midsummer Night's Dream, all I remember about this was a wickedly cool fairy and something about a guy turning into a donkey that I thought was pretty funny. It was not until I started analyzing Shakespeare's plays as an actor that I realized one very important thing, I still didn't understand them. Seriously though, it's tough enough for adults, let alone kids. Then it hit me, why don't I make a version that kids could perform, but make it easy for them to understand with a splash of Shakespeare lingo mixed in? And voila! A melodramatic masterpiece was created! They are intended to be melodramatically fun!

THE PLAYS: There are 3 plays within this book, for three different group sizes. The reason: to allow educators or parents to get the story across to their children regardless of the size of their group. As you read through the plays, there are several lines that are highlighted. These are actual lines from the original book. I am a little more particular about the kids saying these lines verbatim. But the rest, well... have fun!

The entire purpose of this book is to instill the love of a classic story, as well as drama, into the kids.

And when you have children who have a passion for something, they will start to teach themselves, with or without school.

These plays are intended for pure fun. Please DO NOT have the kids learn these lines verbatim, that would be a complete waste of creativity. But do have them basically know their lines and improvise wherever they want as long as it pertains to telling the story. Because that is the goal of an actor: to tell the story. In A Midsummer Night's Dream, I once had a student playing Quince question me about one of her lines, "but in the actual story, didn't the Mechanicals state that 'they would hang us'?" I thought for a second and realized that she had read the story with her mom, and she was right. So I let her add the line she wanted and it added that much more fun, it made the play theirs. I have had kids throw water on the audience, run around the audience, sit in the audience, lose their pumpkin pants (size 30 around a size 15 doesn't work very well, but makes for some great humor!) and most importantly, die all over the stage. The kids love it.

One last note: if you want some educational resources, loved our plays, want to tell the world how much your kids loved performing Shakespeare, want to insult someone with our Shakespeare Insult Generator, or are just a fan of Shakespeare, then hop on our website and have fun:

PlayingWithPlays.com

With these notes, I'll see you on the stage, have fun, and break a leg!

SCHOOL, AFTERSCHOOL, and SUMMER classes

I've been teaching these plays as afterschool and summer programs for quite some time. Many people have asked what the program is, therefore, I have put together a basic formula so any teacher or parent can follow and have melodramatic success! As well, many teachers use my books in a variety of ways. You can view the formula and many more resources on my website at: PlayingWithPlays.com

- Brendan

OTHER PLAYS AND FULL LENGTH SCRIPTS

We have over 25 different titles, as well as a full-length play in 4-acts for theatre groups: Shakespeare's Hilarious Tragedies. You can see all of our other titles on our website here: PlayingWithPlays.com/books

As well, you can see a sneak peek at some of those titles at the back of this book.

And, if you ever have any questions, please don't hesitate to ask at: Contact@PlayingWithPlays.com

ROYALTIES

If you have any questions about royalties or performance licenses, here are the basic guidelines:

1) Please contact us! We always LOVE to hear about a school or group performing our books! We would also love to share photos and brag about your program as well! (with your permission, of course)

2) If you are a group and DO NOT charge your kids to be in this production, contact us about discounted copyright fees (one way or another, we will make this work for you!) You are NOT required to buy a book per kid (but we will still send you some really cool Shakespeare tattoos for your kids!)

3) If you are a group and DO charge your kids to be in the production, (i.e. afterschool program, summer camp) we ask that you purchase a book per kid. Contact us as we will give you a bulk discount (10 books or more) and send some really cool press on Shakespeare tattoos!

4) If you are a group and DO NOT charge the audience to see the plays, please see our website FAQs to see if you are eligible to waive the performance royalties (most performances are eligible).

5) If you are a group and DO charge the audience to see the performance, please see our website FAQs for performance licensing fees (this includes performances for donations and competitions).

Any other questions or comments, please see our website or email us at:

contact@PlayingWithPlays.com

The 15-Minute or so Comedy of Errors
By William Shakespeare
Creatively modified by
Brendan P. Kelso

9 - 12 Actors

CAST OF CHARACTERS:

[1]**DUKE:** Duke of Ephesus

[2]**EGEON:** father looking for his family

ANTIPHOLUS OF SYRACUSE: twin son

DROMIO OF SYRACUSE: another twin, and servant of Antipholus of Syracuse

ANTIPHOLUS OF EPHESUS: twin son

DROMIO OF EPHESUS: yes, another twin, and yes, servant of Antipholus of Ephesus

[3]**LADY ABBESS:** long lost mother of all!

ADRIANA: wife of Antipholus of Ephesus

[3]**LUCIANA:** sister of Adriana

ANGELO: goldsmith, maker of nice bling

[1]**DR. PINCH:** daytime teacher/nighttime conjurer

[2]**MERCHANT:** a merchant with no name

The same actors can play the following part:
[1]DUKE and DR. PINCH
[2]EGEON and MERCHANT
[3]LADY ABESS and LUCIANA

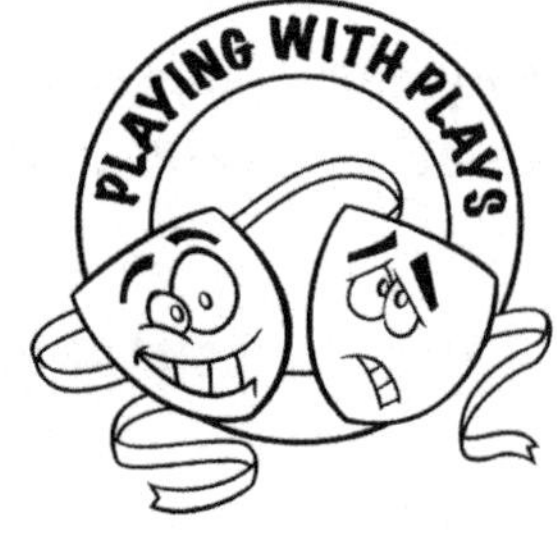

ACT 1 SCENE 1

(DUKE and EGEON enter)

DUKE: You seem like a decent fellow, Egeon. I hate to kill you.

EGEON: You seem like a decent fellow, Duke. I hate to die.

DUKE: Tell me, before I run you through, how did you come to be in our fair city of Ephesus?

EGEON: I came looking for my lost family.

DUKE: So you lost your family and now you're going to lose your life? Rough day.

EGEON: Yes, we had twin boys, but my wife and the boys were separated at sea.

DUKE: Twins, huh?

EGEON: Yes, and THEY had twin servants, who were also separated.

DUKE: Twin servants, for twin boys? Interesting! Confusing, but interesting!

EGEON: It's way more complicated than that, you know, Shakespeare.

DUKE: *(DUKE nods)* Ah, Shakespeare. Keeping people confused since 1590!

EGEON: Exactly. But, to keep it simple, I never found my wife, my other son, or his servant, and now I'm searching the world for them!

DUKE: Touching story. I'll tell you what. Instead of killing you today, I'll kill you tomorrow. A passed sentence may not be recall'd, but I will grant you one day!

EGEON: That is so kind of you!

DUKE: I try. Go! Try to find your family. I know you've failed these past thirty-three years, but something tells me this next twenty-four hours will be different! Go!

EGEON: *(running off)* Thank you! Thank you!!!

DUKE: *(to audience)* I'm such a good duke.

(DUKE exits)

(ANTIPHOLUS S and DROMIO S enter looking like tourists)

ANTIPHOLUS S: Dromio, my servant...

DROMIO S: Yes, master Antipholus?

ANTIPHOLUS S: What is the name of this fair city?

DROMIO S: Ephesus, sir. But, there's a problem.

ANTIPHOLUS S: What problem?

DROMIO S: Well, you know how we are from Syracuse?

ANTIPHOLUS S: Of course.

DROMIO S: Soooo, apparently, anyone from Syracuse has to pay 1,000 gold marks or be executed!

ANTIPHOLUS S: What?!?!

DROMIO S: Yep! I heard some old man was to be executed this morning for this very same thing!

ANTIPHOLUS S: But we are just here to look for my mom and long-lost brother.

DROMIO S: Yeahhhh. But they'll kill us anyway!!!

ANTIPHOLUS S: Well, that's a downer. Doesn't seem to be a very fair city, now, does it?

DROMIO S: No master, it doesn't. What ever shall we do?

(they pause to think)

ANTIPHOLUS S: I have an idea! We can't look like travelers! Take our gear and my money to the Centaur, and get us a room.

DROMIO S: Very well, sir! Center room! But what hotel? *(overloaded with gear, fun chaos ensues as he leaves the stage)*

ANTIPHOLUS S: I just told you. The Centaur.

DROMIO S: Riiiight... Center room.

ANTIPHOLUS S: Noooo. CENTAUR HOTEL. *(acts like horse)*

DROMIO S: Ohhhhh... now that makes more sense.

ANTIPHOLUS S: Now go! *(DROMIO S exits; to audience)* Dromio is crazy. They sure don't make servants like they used to!

(DROMIO E enters opposite)

DROMIO E: There you are, master!

ANTIPHOLUS S: Wow, Dromio, thou art return'd so soon? Didn't you just... *(points opposite)* never mind.

DROMIO E: *(confused)* Return'd so soon? Rather approached too late.

ANTIPHOLUS S: Huh?

DROMIO E: Huh?

ANTIPHOLUS S: *(to audience)* See, my servant is crazy.

DROMIO E: Ummm, your wife sent me. Dinner is ready, and she wants you home now!

ANTIPHOLUS S: What in the world are you talking about?

DROMIO E: Ummm... happy wife, happy life?

ANTIPHOLUS S: Which I agree with. But you were supposed to deliver my luggage, not get me a wife. Now quit being a fool. Where have you left the money?

DROMIO E: Money?

ANTIPHOLUS S: Yes! My thousand gold marks! My possessions! I'm about to get mad. Big and ugly mad! Tell me, where is my money?

DROMIO E: Possessions? You mean your wife, right?

ANTIPHOLUS S: *(to audience)* Crazy!!!

ADRIANA: *(backstage)* I am no one's possession!

DROMIO E: There's your love now!

ANTIPHOLUS S: What in the world...

DROMIO E: You really are strange right now, sir.

ANTIPHOLUS S: I'm strange? You're the one saying I'm married. And where have you bestow'd my money?!

DROMIO E: *(slowly starts stepping back)* You are married and there is no money.

ANTIPHOLUS S: WHAT!!!!

(DROMIO E runs offstage)

ANTIPHOLUS S: Dark-working sorcerers have changed his mind!!! This town is full of cozenage! Trickery abounds! *(runs off opposite)*

<h1 style="text-align:center">ACT 2 SCENE I</h1>

(enter ADRIANA and LUCIANA)

ADRIANA: Where is Antipholus? Neither my husband nor the slave return'd. Dinner is getting cold!

LUCIANA: Adriana, be patient sister, and wait for your husband. You need to be a good wife.

ADRIANA: I'm sorry, what? Luciana, are you wedded?

LUCIANA: Ah, no...

ADRIANA: That's right, you're not. I'm no homemaker! He does NOT control me. Bite your tongue till the day YOU have a husband!

LUCIANA: I'm just saying, this is the 1600s, women don't have any rights.

ADRIANA: Well, we'll just see about that!

(enter DROMIO E)

ADRIANA: Where is my husband!?

DROMIO E: Well, ma'am, he's acting REALLY weird and keeps saying, "No house, no wife... My gold! My gold!"

ADRIANA: *(grabs DROMIO'S ear)* Go back again and fetch him home.

DROMIO E: But he'll be mad! Please, send some other messenger!

ADRIANA: Back, Dromio, or I will break your head.

DROMIO E: I'll fetch thy master! *(exits)*

ADRIANA: And don't return without him!

DROMIO E: *(offstage)* Yes ma'am!

ADRIANA: *(to LUCIANA)* Servants these days.

(ALL exit)

<h1 align="center">ACT 2 SCENE 2</h1>

(enter ANTIPHOLUS S)

ANTIPHOLUS S: *(to audience)* I was furious! So, I went to speak with the innkeeper at The Centaur. And, strangely enough, apparently Dromio DID leave our luggage, and my money there.

(enter DROMIO S)

ANTIPHOLUS S: YOU!

DROMIO S: ME!

ANTIPHOLUS S: Don't 'me', me!

DROMIO S: Huh? Why would I 'you', you?

ANTIPHOLUS S: Why did you lie to me?

DROMIO S: Huh?

ANTIPHOLUS S: All this nonsense about a mistress and a dinner!

DROMIO S: Huh?

ANTIPHOLUS S: You did just what I asked!

DROMIO S: Right.

ANTIPHOLUS S: Right!

DROMIO S: Soooo...

ANTIPHOLUS S: Soooo... I'm confused. Know any good jokes?

DROMIO S: Of course! Why did the chicken cross the playground?

ANTIPHOLUS S: Ummm, dunno.

DROMIO S: To get to the other SLIDE!

(they laugh)

DROMIO S: Okay, okay... what do you call a fake noodle?

ANTIPHOLUS S: I don't know.

DROMIO S: Impasta!!!

(they laugh; enter ADRIANA and LUCIANA, they stare for a moment, then ADRIANA coughs expectantly)

ADRIANA: Ay, Ay, Antipholus, wipe that silly smirk off your face.

ANTIPHOLUS S: I'm sorry, I know you not.

ADRIANA: Excuse me?

LUCIANA: Fie, brother! How dare you talk to your wife that way?

ADRIANA: I can handle this, Luciana. How dare you talk to your wife that way?!

LUCIANA: Yeah!

ANTIPHOLUS S: More of this wife stuff? What is going on here?

LUCIANA: She sent for you by Dromio home to dinner.

ANTIPHOLUS S: By Dromio?

DROMIO S: What?! By me?

ADRIANA & LUCIANA: YES!

DROMIO S: Who are these chicks?

ADRIANA: Chicks?

DROMIO S: Sorry. Babes.

LUCIANA: Babes?!

DROMIO S: I think the lady doth protest too much!

(MEN laugh)

ADRIANA: That's it! Come back home, now!

(grabs their ears and drags them offstage; ALL exit, then return still dragging them by their ears; she lets go)

ANTIPHOLUS S: Okay, okay... I'll be your husband, sheesh.

ADRIANA: That's more like it.

LUCIANA: Yeah! What she said.

ADRIANA: Dromio, guard this door. You, *(pointing at ANTIPHOLUS S)* let's go eat!

ANTIPHOLUS S: *(to DROMIO)* Well, at least I get a meal out of it.

(ALL exit)

ACT 3 SCENE 1

(ANTIPHOLUS E, DROMIO E, and ANGELO enter)

ANTIPHOLUS E: Angelo, I'll have my wife make us a great meal. Dromio, open the gates for us.

DROMIO E: Yes, master Antipholus.

ANGELO: I'm looking forward to this great meal, Antipholus. Your wife's cooking is the best!

ANTIPHOLUS E: It is. It is. What is taking so long, Dromio?

DROMIO E: It is locked.

ANTIPHOLUS E: Well, knock on it, you fool!

(DROMIO "knocks" on door)

DROMIO S: *(offstage)* Yes?

DROMIO E: Let us in!

DROMIO S: No!

DROMIO E: Sir, apparently, they won't let us in.

ANTIPHOLUS E: What?! *("knocks")*

DROMIO S: Yes?

ANTIPHOLUS E: I demand you to let us in!

DROMIO S: No!

ANTIPHOLUS E: WHAT?! I am the master of this house. Let us in!

DROMIO S: Ummm... No?

ANTIPHOLUS E: WHAT?! LET US IN NOWWWWWWWW!!!

DROMIO S: Sorry, the master says no!

ANTIPHOLUS E: I AM the master!!!

DROMIO S: Riiiiight.

DROMIO E: Keep knocking, master!

DROMIO S: You can knock till it ache. Goodbye!

ANTIPHOLUS E: Let's break down the door!

ANGELO: Perhaps we should not.

ANTIPHOLUS E: What?!

ANGELO: Well, maybe your wife has a reason for keeping you out?

ANTIPHOLUS E: A reason?

ANGELO: Yes! Maybe she's planning a surprise party!

ANTIPHOLUS E: My birthday is not for another six months!

ANGELO: She's a planner?

ANTIPHOLUS E: Arghh! Let's just go into town. I'll clear this up tomorrow.

ANGELO: Sounds good.

ANTIPHOLUS E: By the way, Angelo, can you make me a gold chain? I need something to make me happy.

ANGELO: You got it! I'll bring it by tomorrow.

ANTIPHOLUS E: Great! To the town!

(ALL exit)

(enter ANTIPHOLUS S and LUCIANA a moment later yelling)

LUCIANA: I can't believe you are treating my sister, YOUR WIFE, with such disrespect!

ANTIPHOLUS S: Sweet mistress, in my defense...

LUCIANA: Don't sweet mistress me! Enough of the insolence! You have been childish, rude, arrogant, and vain.

ANTIPHOLUS S: Wow. You're feisty!

LUCIANA: Excuse me?!

ANTIPHOLUS S: *(grabs his heart)* Wait! What's that feeling? Oh, no! I think I just fell in love with you!

LUCIANA: What?! Are you mad?! You can't say that!!!

ANTIPHOLUS S: It's Shakespeare, sure I can!

LUCIANA: Arghhhh!!!! Adriana!!! Your husband just told me he loves me! *(exits yelling)*

ANTIPHOLUS S: Oh, no! No, no, nooo... oh well. *(to audience)* I like her!

(enter DROMIO S)

DROMIO S: Hey boss! Get this: the lady that runs the kitchen, thinks I'm her husband!

ANTIPHOLUS S: What? What is it with all these women?

DROMIO S: Not sure. Don't you think it's really weird that she thinks I'm her husband and Adriana thinks you're her husband?

ANTIPHOLUS S: Totally! I mean, what are the odds of BOTH of them mistaking us for their spouses?

DROMIO S: Hold on. This is too coincidental.

ANTIPHOLUS S: Are you thinking what I'm thinking?

DROMIO S: I think so!

ANTIPHOLUS S: That we should get the heck out of this town because witches do inhabit here?

DROMIO S: Exactly!!!

ANTIPHOLUS S: Great, go down to the docks and book passage to leave tonight.

DROMIO S: I'm on it!

(DROMIO S exits)

ANTIPHOLUS S: *(to audience)* But, Luciana! Her beauty, and feistiness, make me never want to leave! Buuuut... on the other hand... witches. Oh! I have been enchanted!

(enter ANGELO)

ANGELO: Master Antipholus.

ANTIPHOLUS S: Ay, that's my name.

ANGELO: Here is the gold chain. I have made it for you. *(puts it on ANTIPHOLUS)*

ANTIPHOLUS S: Made it for me? I didn't request it.

ANGELO: That looks gooood! Payment? *(puts hand out)*

ANTIPHOLUS S: What? I don't want any necklace! And I don't have any money!

ANGELO: Just pay me later! Fare you well! *(exits)*

ANTIPHOLUS S: But I didn't order it! This town is bonkers. *(examines it; to audience)* Although, I do make it look good! Maybe I will keep it. *(exits)*

(ANGELO enters, MERCHANT enters opposite)

MERCHANT: Angelo! I'm glad to see you. I need the money you owe me.

ANGELO: Yeah... about that. Antipholus owes me that exact amount by five o'clock. Once I collect, I will pay you back!

MERCHANT: You better. I wouldn't want to "collect" some other way.

ANGELO: You and me both!

(enter ANTIPHOLUS E and DROMIO E)

DROMIO E: Sir, that was a chilly night. Are we going home today?

ANTIPHOLUS E: Yes, we will. In the meantime, go get me donuts. I like donuts.

DROMIO E: Donuts! Yes, sir! *(exits)*

(ANGELO coughs expectantly)

ANTIPHOLUS E: Angelo! Sorry about dinner last night.

ANGELO: That's okay. How about you give me the money you owe me for the gold chain I made you? I stand debted to this gentleman.

ANTIPHOLUS E: I'm sorry, what?

ANGELO: The gold chain. I gave it to you at your house. Just an hour ago. I need the money.

ANTIPHOLUS E: My house? Gave me a gold chain? Whatever are you talking about?

ANGELO: *(getting angry)* Very funny, Antipholus. The money... now.

ANTIPHOLUS E: There was no chain and you're not getting any money.

ANGELO: Really?

MERCHANT: I have an idea. *(grabs ANTIPHOLUS' arm, yells offstage)* OFFICER!

ANTIPHOLUS E: What are you doing?

MERCHANT: I'm having you arrested!

ANTIPHOLUS E: This is ridiculous!

(DROMIO S enters)

DROMIO S: Sir, ummm... you're being arrested.

ANTIPHOLUS E: Really?! I didn't notice!

DROMIO S: By the way, I have secured passage on a ship!

ANTIPHOLUS E: What?! Man, you have been acting really weird lately! I'm tired of your antics. I asked for donuts, NOT A SHIP!

DROMIO S: Donuts?

ANTIPHOLUS E: Forget the donuts! Go to my wife, get money, so I can give thee bail!

DROMIO S: Money. Bail. Right! And... what about the ship?

ANTIPHOLUS E: Forget the ship! Forget the donuts! Man, you are dense!

DROMIO S: No ship! No donuts!

ANTIPHOLUS E: GO!!!

(ALL exit; moments later ADRIANA and LUCIANA enter)

LUCIANA: Adriana, you need to know this! Your husband told me he loved me! He is deranged! No... posses'd!

ADRIANA: Say what now?! What did you do?!

LUCIANA: Nothing! Except for being gorgeous, of course!

ADRIANA: Of course! That fool! Why do I love him so?!

(enter DROMIO S)

DROMIO S: Hello again!

ADRIANA: Where is thy master, Dromio?

DROMIO S: Ummm... your husband's been arrested and needs money.

ADRIANA: What, is he arrested?

DROMIO S: Uh, yeah, that's what I just said.

ADRIANA: What is going on with that fool?!

LUCIANA: Told you, deranged AND possess'd!

ADRIANA: Go, Dromio; there's the money. Keep my fool out of jail!

DROMIO S: Yes, ma'am!

(ALL exit)

(ANTIPHOLUS S enters)

ANTIPHOLUS S: *(to audience)* The people in this town are soooo nice! Totally weird, but nice. The weird thing? They all know my name. Strange, right?

(enter DROMIO S breathing heavy)

DROMIO S: Sir! Your money!

ANTIPHOLUS S: What money?! I didn't ask for any money.

DROMIO S: You know, bail for jail? You've been arrested...

ANTIPHOLUS S: Jail?! Arrested?! Man, you are going insane, too. What about the ship? Did you find us a ship to leave on?

DROMIO S: Ship?! You told me to forget about the ship. AND the donuts!

ANTIPHOLUS S: Donuts? I told you what?! This place is surely possessed! We need to leave soon!

(ALL exit)

(enter ANTIPHOLUS E and DROMIO E)

DROMIO E: Here are the donuts you asked for, sir!

ANTIPHOLUS E: *(angry)* Donuts?! I don't need donuts; I need money to stay out of jail! But, I do like donuts. Give me those.

DROMIO E: Jail? Why are you going to jail?

ANTIPHOLUS E: Why, I oughta...

(ANTIPHOLUS E throws donut at DROMIO E, then chases around stage, stops abruptly when PINCH, ADRIANA, and LUCIANA enter)

ADRIANA: Dr. Pinch, I need you to take my husband, and his wacky servant, and get rid of the demons within them!

PINCH, DROMIO E, & ANTIPHOLUS E: DEMONS?!

ANTIPHOLUS E: Woah, wifey-poo, I ain't got no demons!

DROMIO E: And I'm not wacky!

ADRIANA: Quiet!!!

ANTIPHOLUS E: *(aside to DROMIO)* You are kind of wacky.

PINCH: Listen, lady, I'm only doing this sorcery gig as a side business because they don't pay me enough as a schoolteacher.

ADRIANA: Wait, but you're a doctor?

PINCH: Yes, but a doctor of history. So...

ADRIANA: Ohhhh... so... schoolteacher, I get it. Well, I don't care. Just do it!

PINCH: Okay, okay... pushy, pushy. But if they go crazy, I'm out of here!

ADRIANA: Fine, just get them!

PINCH: Both man and master is possess'd! Come here you two!

(chaos ensues; ANTIPHOLUS E and DROMIO E are tied up by PINCH)

PINCH: To the basement! The fiend is strong within them.

(ANTIPHOLUS E and DROMIO E are led offstage by PINCH)

ANTIPHOLUS E: *(exiting)* I am not mad I tell you!!! NOT MAD!

DROMIO E: And I'm not wacky!

LUCIANA: Oh, he is definitely mad!

ADRIANA: Whew! I'm finally glad they're gone.

(ANTIPHOLUS S and DROMIO S enter opposite)

ANTIPHOLUS S: Hello!

ADRIANA: For thy mercy! They are loose again.

LUCIANA: Let's get out of here!

(ADRIANA and LUCIANA exit screaming)

DROMIO S: Huh. Must have been something you said.

ANTIPHOLUS S: This place is insane! Fetch our stuff and let's leave tonight.

DROMIO S: Agreed!

(ALL exit)

<h1 style="text-align:center">ACT 5 SCENE 1</h1>

(enter ANGELO)

ANGELO: *(to audience)* Antipholus has a great reputation, is highly beloved, and wealthy! But, I need that money. Here he comes now. And he's wearing the chain about his neck!

(enter ANTIPHOLUS S and DROMIO S)

ANTIPHOLUS S: Dromio, we need to get out of here soon!

ANGELO: YOU! I demand payment.

DROMIO S: Very soon. This town is absolutely cuckoo!

ANGELO: I do defy thee for a villain.

ANTIPHOLUS S: How dare you call me a villain!

(ALL draw swords and prepare to fight; pause, then ADRIANA enters)

DROMIO S: The crazy lady approaches.

ADRIANA: There you are! Take his sword away!

DROMIO S: Run, master, run! Into the priory!

(ANTIPHOLUS S and DROMIO S exit)

ADRIANA: Stop!

(ADRIANA follows but can't "enter")

ADRIANA: It is locked!

(enter ABBESS)

ABBESS: Hello. May I help you?

ADRIANA: Yes! My loony husband is in there. I demand you let him out!

ABBESS: He is only loony because you are a jealous, and loud, woman.

ADRIANA: WHAT!?! I AM NOT... jealous.

ABBESS: I will cure what ails him. Now leave. Not a creature enters in my house. Good day. *(exits)*

ADRIANA: Who does she think she is?!

ANGELO: You ARE kind of loud sometimes...

ADRIANA: I AM NOT! Achemm... I am not. I have a firm voice.

ANGELO: Okay...

(enter DUKE and EGEON; all kneel)

DUKE: Egeon, the time has come. *(to audience)* I need to proclaim it publicly. If any friend shall pay the sum for him, he shall not die. *(silence)* Very well. Tough luck, Egeon.

EGEON: Yes, luck. I need just a bit more of it.

ADRIANA: Justice, most sacred duke, against the abbess!

DUKE: I'm sorry, what? Can't you see I'm about to behead someone?

EGEON: No, no. Go on about your business. I'm good.

DUKE: Very well.

ADRIANA: The abbess is holding my husband captive! Demand she lets him go!

DUKE: Your husband has served me well over the years. I shall help. *(approaches priory)*

(ANGELO looks and points offstage)

ANGELO: O mistress, mistress, your husband and his man are both broke loose.

ADRIANA: Peace, fool! Thy master and his man are here.

ANGELO: Then who are they?!

(enter ANTIPHOLUS E and DROMIO E)

ALL: What?!!!

ADRIANA: Ay me, it is my husband! You see that, right?

ANGELO: *(nodding confused)* Uh, huh.

ANTIPHOLUS E: This has been the strangest day, ever!

DROMIO E: Yes, it has!

EGEON: *(to audience)* What luck! Unless the fear of death doth make me dote, I see my son Antipholus and Dromio.

ADRIANA: *(to ANTIPHOLUS E)* Who are you?!

ANTIPHOLUS E: I am your husband, dear woman!

ADRIANA: Are not!

ANTIPHOLUS E: Are too!

ADRIANA: Nope! My husband is in there! *(points offstage)* I think.

DUKE: What is going on here?!

ANTIPHOLUS E: This WOMAN has locked me out of my house. The goldsmith accused me of stealing a chain. The merchant had me arrested. And then Pinch, a hungry lean-faced villain, cries out, I was possess'd! Bounded me and tossed me into the basement!

DROMIO E: Me too!

ADRIANA: Clearly you ARE possess'd, because my husband is in there!

DUKE: Stop! You saw'st him enter the abbey here?

ADRIANA: Yes!

DUKE: *(to ANGELO)* You! Go in and fetch the abbess.

(ANGELO exits; EGEON hugs ANTIPHOLUS E, who goes stiff, and pries off hug)

ANTIPHOLUS E: What is this? Who is this old man?

EGEON: Sir, are you call'd Antipholus? And your bondman, Dromio?

ANTIPHOLUS E: Maybe...

EGEON: Then you know me well. I am your father.

ALL: What?!!!

ANTIPHOLUS E: I never saw my father in my life.

DROMIO E: Truth!

EGEON: It's only been seven years since Syracuse. Surely you remember me?

ANTIPHOLUS E: Strange, old man, I've never been to Syracuse.

(enter ANGELO, ABBESS, ANTIPHOLUS S, and DROMIO S)

ABBESS: Most mighty duke, behold a man much wrong'd.

ADRIANA: I see two husbands, or mine eyes deceive me.

ANTIPHOLUS S: Dad?!

EGEON: Son! *(they embrace)*

DROMIO S: Old master! *(hugs them both)* Who hath bound him here?

ABBESS: Whoever bound him, I will loose his bonds. For, he has just gained a wife.

ALL: WHAT?!!!

ABBESS: Tis true! My name is Emilia, and we once had two fair sons.

EGEON: Dear Emilia! *(they hug)* But what happened to our son?

ABBESS: Antipholus and his servant, Dromio, were forced from me when we washed to shore. I had not seen them since, well... today.

ANTIPHOLUS S & E: Mom?!

ABBESS: Sons! *(all hug)*

ADRIANA: I've got a mother-in-law?

ANTIPHOLUS E: Mom, this is my wife, Adriana.

ABBESS: Bring it in, daughter! *(they hug)*

ANGELO: And the gold chain?

ANTIPHOLUS S: Oh, yes. This must be yours then. *(hands ANTIPHOLUS E chain)*

ANTIPHOLUS E: And this must be your money. *(pays ANGELO)*

ANGELO: Great!

ANTIPHOLUS E: These ducats pawn I for my father here.

DUKE: It shall not need; thy father hath his life.

ALL: Yay!

ABBESS: Great! It's been thirty-three years, time to party!

DUKE: With all my heart, I'll gossip at this feast.

ANTIPHOLUS S: Well, this is a great ending! *(sees ANTIPHOLUS E, claps his shoulder)* Embrace thy brother. *(they hug)*

ANTIPHOLUS E: Ready to party?

ANTIPHOLUS S: Absolutely!

(ALL exit except the DROMIOS)

DROMIO S: *(looking at DROMIO E)* Man, I am good-looking!

DROMIO E: Yes, you are!

DROMIO S: Let's go celebrate!

DROMIO E: Yes! Let's go hand in hand, not one before another.

(they link arms and exit)

THE END

The 20-Minute or so Comedy of Errors

By William Shakespeare
Creatively modified by
Brendan P. Kelso

11 - 16+ Actors

CAST OF CHARACTERS:

[1]**DUKE**: Duke of Ephesus

[2]**EGEON**: father looking for his family

ANTIPHOLUS OF SYRACUSE: twin son

DROMIO OF SYRACUSE: another twin, and servant of Antipholus of Syracuse

ANTIPHOLUS OF EPHESUS: twin son

DROMIO OF EPHESUS: yes, another twin, and yes, servant of Antipholus of Ephesus

[3]**LADY ABBESS**: long lost mother of all!

ADRIANA: wife of Antipholus of Ephesus

LUCIANA: sister of Adriana

ANGELO: goldsmith, maker of nice bling

[4]**BALTHASAR**: a merchant with an actual name

[1]**INNKEEPER**: the keeper of inns

[4]**OFFICER**: keeper of the law

[2]**DR. PINCH**: daytime teacher/nighttime conjurer

[3]**MERCHANT**: a merchant with no name

TOWNSFOLK: a person from town

The same actors can play the following part:
[1]DUKE and INNKEEPER
[2]EGEON and DR. PINCH
[3]LADY ABESS and MERCHANT
[4]BALTHASAR and OFFICER
TOWNSFOLK can be extras and randomly inserted throughout play

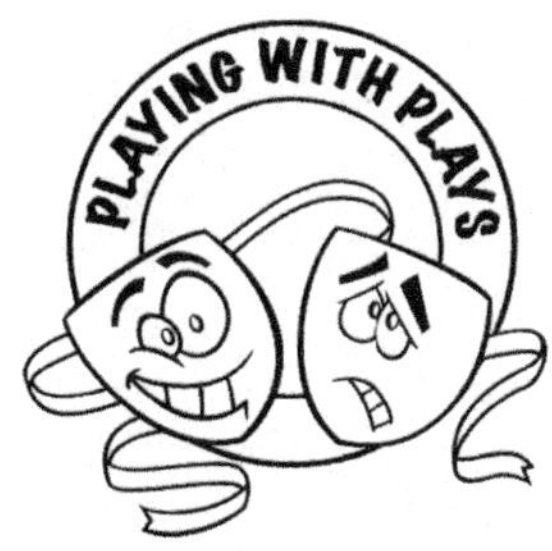

ACT 1 SCENE 1

(DUKE and EGEON enter)

DUKE: You seem like a decent fellow, Egeon. I hate to kill you.

EGEON: You seem like a decent fellow, Duke. I hate to die.

DUKE: Tell me, before I run you through, how did you come to be in our fair city of Ephesus?

EGEON: I came looking for my lost family.

DUKE: So you lost your family and now you're going to lose your life? Rough day.

EGEON: Yes, we had twin boys, but my wife and the boys were separated at sea.

DUKE: Twins, huh?

EGEON: Yes, and THEY had twin servants, who were also separated.

DUKE: Twin servants, for twin boys? Interesting! Confusing, but interesting!

EGEON: It's way more complicated than that, you know, Shakespeare.

DUKE: *(DUKE nods)* Ah, Shakespeare. Keeping people confused since 1590!

EGEON: Exactly. But, to keep it simple, I never found my wife, my other son, or his servant, and now I'm searching the world for them!

DUKE: Touching story. I'll tell you what. Instead of killing you today, I'll kill you tomorrow. A passed sentence may not be recall'd, but I will grant you one day!

EGEON: That is so kind of you!

DUKE: I try. Go! Try to find your family. I know you've failed these past thirty-three years, but something tells me this next twenty-four hours will be different! Go!

EGEON: *(running off)* Thank you! Thank you!!!

DUKE: *(to audience)* I'm such a good duke.

(DUKE exits)

(ANTIPHOLUS S and DROMIO S enter looking like tourists)

ANTIPHOLUS S: Dromio, my servant...

DROMIO S: Yes, master Antipholus?

ANTIPHOLUS S: What is the name of this fair city?

DROMIO S: Ephesus, sir. But, there's a problem.

ANTIPHOLUS S: What problem?

DROMIO S: Well, you know how we are from Syracuse?

ANTIPHOLUS S: Of course.

DROMIO S: Soooo, apparently, anyone from Syracuse has to pay 1,000 gold marks or be executed!

ANTIPHOLUS S: What?!?!

DROMIO S: Yep! I heard some old man was to be executed this morning for this very same thing!

ANTIPHOLUS S: But we are just here to look for my mom and long-lost brother.

DROMIO S: Yeahhhh. But they'll kill us anyway!!!

ANTIPHOLUS S: Well, that's a downer. Doesn't seem to be a very fair city, now, does it?

DROMIO S: No master, it doesn't. What ever shall we do?

(they pause to think)

ANTIPHOLUS S: I have an idea! We can't look like travelers! Take our gear and my money to the Centaur, and get us a room.

DROMIO S: Very well, sir! Center room! But what hotel? *(overloaded with gear, fun chaos ensues as he leaves the stage)*

ANTIPHOLUS S: I just told you. The Centaur.

DROMIO S: Riiiight... Center room.

ANTIPHOLUS S: Noooo. CENTAUR HOTEL. *(acts like horse)*

DROMIO S: Ohhhhh... now that makes more sense.

ANTIPHOLUS S: Now go! *(DROMIO S exits; to audience)* Dromio is crazy. They sure don't make servants like they used to!

(DROMIO E enters opposite)

DROMIO E: There you are, master!

ANTIPHOLUS S: Wow, Dromio, thou art return'd so soon? Didn't you just... *(points opposite)* never mind.

DROMIO E: *(confused)* Return'd so soon? Rather approached too late.

ANTIPHOLUS S: Huh?

DROMIO E: Huh?

ANTIPHOLUS S: *(to audience)* See, my servant is crazy.

DROMIO E: Ummm, your wife sent me. Dinner is ready, and she wants you home now!

ANTIPHOLUS S: What in the world are you talking about?

DROMIO E: Ummm... happy wife, happy life?

ANTIPHOLUS S: Which I agree with. But you were supposed to deliver my luggage, not get me a wife. Now quit being a fool. Where have you left the money?

DROMIO E: Money?

ANTIPHOLUS S: Yes! My thousand gold marks! My possessions! I'm about to get mad. Big and ugly mad! Tell me, where is my money?

DROMIO E: Possessions? You mean your wife, right?

ANTIPHOLUS S: *(to audience)* Crazy!!!

ADRIANA: *(backstage)* I am no one's possession!

DROMIO E: There's your love now!

ANTIPHOLUS S: What in the world...

DROMIO E: You really are strange right now, sir.

ANTIPHOLUS S: I'm strange? You're the one saying I'm married. And where have you bestow'd my money?!

DROMIO E: *(slowly starts stepping back)* You are married and there is no money.

ANTIPHOLUS S: WHAT!!!!

(DROMIO E runs offstage)

ANTIPHOLUS S: Dark-working sorcerers have changed his mind!!! This town is full of cozenage! Trickery abounds! *(runs off opposite)*

ACT 2 SCENE I

(enter ADRIANA and LUCIANA)

ADRIANA: Where is Antipholus? Neither my husband nor the slave return'd. Dinner is getting cold!

LUCIANA: Adriana, be patient sister, and wait for your husband. You need to be a good wife.

ADRIANA: I'm sorry, what? Luciana, are you wedded?

LUCIANA: Ah, no...

ADRIANA: That's right, you're not. I'm no homemaker! He does NOT control me. Bite your tongue till the day YOU have a husband!

LUCIANA: I'm just saying, this is the 1600s, women don't have any rights.

ADRIANA: Well, we'll just see about that!

(enter DROMIO E)

ADRIANA: Where is my husband!?

DROMIO E: Well, ma'am, he's acting REALLY weird and keeps saying, "No house, no wife... My gold! My gold!"

ADRIANA: *(grabs DROMIO'S ear)* Go back again and fetch him home.

DROMIO E: But he'll be mad! Please, send some other messenger!

ADRIANA: Back, Dromio, or I will break your head.

DROMIO E: I'll fetch thy master! *(exits)*

ADRIANA: And don't return without him!

DROMIO E: *(offstage)* Yes ma'am!

ADRIANA: *(to LUCIANA)* Servants these days.

(ALL exit)

(enter ANTIPHOLUS S and INNKEEPER)

ANTIPHOLUS S: *(to audience)* Let's see what that bold-faced liar actually did with my money! *(to INNKEEPER)* Hello innkeeper, I was wondering if my luggage was dropped off earlier?

INNKEEPER: Yes! And a thousand gold marks as well. It's all stored in the back.

ANTIPHOLUS S: Really? Okay... thanks.

(INNKEEPER exits)

ANTIPHOLUS S: Well, that is strange.

(enter DROMIO S)

ANTIPHOLUS S: YOU!

DROMIO S: ME!

ANTIPHOLUS S: Don't 'me', me!

DROMIO S: Huh? Why would I 'you', you?

ANTIPHOLUS S: Why did you lie to me?

DROMIO S: Huh?

ANTIPHOLUS S: All this nonsense about a mistress and a dinner!

DROMIO S: Huh?

ANTIPHOLUS S: You did just what I asked!

DROMIO S: Right.

ANTIPHOLUS S: Right!

DROMIO S: Soooo...

ANTIPHOLUS S: Soooo... I'm confused. Know any good jokes?

DROMIO S: Of course! Why did the chicken cross the playground?

ANTIPHOLUS S: Ummm, dunno.

DROMIO S: To get to the other SLIDE!

(they laugh)

DROMIO S: Okay, okay... what do you call a fake noodle?

ANTIPHOLUS S: I don't know.

DROMIO S: Impasta!!!

(they laugh; enter ADRIANA and LUCIANA, they stare for a moment, then ADRIANA coughs expectantly)

ADRIANA: Ay, Ay, Antipholus, wipe that silly smirk off your face.

ANTIPHOLUS S: I'm sorry, I know you not.

ADRIANA: Excuse me?

LUCIANA: Fie, brother! How dare you talk to your wife that way?

ADRIANA: I can handle this, Luciana. How dare you talk to your wife that way?!

LUCIANA: Yeah!

ANTIPHOLUS S: More of this wife stuff? What is going on here?

LUCIANA: She sent for you by Dromio home to dinner.

ANTIPHOLUS S: By Dromio?

DROMIO S: What?! By me?

ADRIANA & LUCIANA: YES!

DROMIO S: Who are these chicks?

ADRIANA: Chicks?

DROMIO S: Sorry. Babes.

LUCIANA: Babes?!

DROMIO S: I think the lady doth protest too much!

(MEN laugh)

ADRIANA: That's it! Come back home, now!

(grabs their ears and drags them offstage; ALL exit, then return still dragging them by their ears; she lets go)

ANTIPHOLUS S: Okay, okay... I'll be your husband, sheesh.

ADRIANA: That's more like it.

LUCIANA: Yeah! What she said.

ADRIANA: Dromio, guard this door. You, *(pointing at ANTIPHOLUS S)* let's go eat!

ANTIPHOLUS S: *(to DROMIO)* Well, at least I get a meal out of it.

(ALL exit)

(ANTIPHOLUS E, DROMIO E, BALTHASAR, and ANGELO enter)

ANTIPHOLUS E: Angelo, Balthasar, I'll have my wife make us a great meal. Dromio, open the gates for us.

DROMIO E: Yes, master Antipholus.

BALTHASAR: I'm looking forward to this great meal, Antipholus.

ANGELO: Your wife's cooking is the best!

ANTIPHOLUS E: It is. It is. What is taking so long, Dromio?

DROMIO E: It is locked.

ANTIPHOLUS E: Well, knock on it, you fool!

(DROMIO "knocks" on door)

DROMIO S: *(offstage)* Yes?

DROMIO E: Let us in!

DROMIO S: No!

DROMIO E: Sir, apparently, they won't let us in.

ANTIPHOLUS E: What?! *("knocks")*

DROMIO S: Yes?

ANTIPHOLUS E: I demand you to let us in!

DROMIO S: No!

ANTIPHOLUS E: WHAT?! I am the master of this house. Let us in!

DROMIO S: Ummm... No?

ANTIPHOLUS E: WHAT?! LET US IN NOWWWWWWW!!!

DROMIO S: Sorry, the master says no!

ANTIPHOLUS E: I AM the master!!!

DROMIO S: Riiiiight.

DROMIO E: Keep knocking, master!

DROMIO S: You can knock till it ache. Goodbye!

ANTIPHOLUS E: Let's break down the door!

BALTHASAR: Perhaps we should not.

ANTIPHOLUS E: What?!

BALTHASAR: Well, maybe your wife has a reason for keeping you out?

ANTIPHOLUS E: A reason?

ANGELO: Yes! Maybe she's planning a surprise party!

ANTIPHOLUS E: My birthday is not for another six months!

ANGELO: She's a planner?

ANTIPHOLUS E: Arghh! Let's just go into town. I'll clear this up tomorrow.

BALTHASAR: Sounds good.

ANTIPHOLUS E: By the way, Angelo, can you make me a gold chain? I need something to make me happy.

ANGELO: You got it! I'll bring it by tomorrow.

ANTIPHOLUS E: Great! To the town!

(ALL exit)

(enter ANTIPHOLUS S and LUCIANA a moment later yelling)

LUCIANA: I can't believe you are treating my sister, YOUR WIFE, with such disrespect!

ANTIPHOLUS S: Sweet mistress, in my defense...

LUCIANA: Don't sweet mistress me! Enough of the insolence! You have been childish, rude, arrogant, and vain.

ANTIPHOLUS S: Wow. You're feisty!

LUCIANA: Excuse me?!

ANTIPHOLUS S: *(grabs his heart)* Wait! What's that feeling? Oh, no! I think I just fell in love with you!

LUCIANA: What?! Are you mad?! You can't say that!!!

ANTIPHOLUS S: It's Shakespeare, sure I can!

LUCIANA: Arghhhh!!!! Adriana!!! Your husband just told me he loves me! *(exits yelling)*

ANTIPHOLUS S: Oh, no! No, no, nooo... oh well. *(to audience)* I like her!

(enter DROMIO S)

DROMIO S: Hey boss! Get this: The lady that runs the kitchen, thinks I'm her husband!

ANTIPHOLUS S: What? What is it with all these women?

DROMIO S: Not sure. Don't you think it's really weird that she thinks I'm her husband and Adriana thinks you're her husband?

ANTIPHOLUS S: Totally! I mean, what are the odds of BOTH of them mistaking us for their spouses?

DROMIO S: Hold on. This is too coincidental.

ANTIPHOLUS S: Are you thinking what I'm thinking?

DROMIO S: I think so!

ANTIPHOLUS S: That we should get the heck out of this town because witches do inhabit here?

DROMIO S: Exactly!!!

ANTIPHOLUS S: Great, go down to the docks and book passage to leave tonight.

DROMIO S: I'm on it!

(DROMIO S exits)

ANTIPHOLUS S: *(to audience)* But, Luciana! Her beauty, and feistiness, make me never want to leave! Buuuut... on the other hand... witches. Oh! I have been enchanted!

(enter ANGELO)

ANGELO: Master Antipholus.

ANTIPHOLUS S: Ay, that's my name.

ANGELO: Here is the gold chain. I have made it for you. *(puts it on ANTIPHOLUS)*

ANTIPHOLUS S: Made it for me? I didn't request it.

ANGELO: That looks gooood! Payment? *(puts hand out)*

ANTIPHOLUS S: What? I don't want any necklace! And I don't have any money!

ANGELO: Just pay me later! Fare you well! *(exits)*

ANTIPHOLUS S: But I didn't order it! This town is bonkers. *(examines it; to audience)* Although, I do make it look good! Maybe I will keep it. *(exits)*

ACT 4 SCENES 1 & 2

(ANGELO enters, MERCHANT enters opposite)

MERCHANT: Angelo! I'm glad to see you. I need the money you owe me.

ANGELO: Yeah... about that. Antipholus owes me that exact amount by five o'clock. Once I collect, I will pay you back!

MERCHANT: You better. I wouldn't want to "collect" some other way.

ANGELO: You and me both!

(enter ANTIPHOLUS E and DROMIO E)

DROMIO E: Sir, that was a chilly night. Are we going home today?

ANTIPHOLUS E: Yes, we will. In the meantime, go get me donuts. I like donuts.

DROMIO E: Donuts! Yes, sir! *(exits)*

(ANGELO coughs expectantly)

ANTIPHOLUS E: Angelo! Sorry about dinner last night.

ANGELO: That's okay. How about you give me the money you owe me for the gold chain I made you? I stand debted to this gentleman.

ANTIPHOLUS E: I'm sorry, what?

ANGELO: The gold chain. I gave it to you at your house. Just an hour ago. I need the money.

ANTIPHOLUS E: My house? Gave me a gold chain? Whatever are you talking about?

ANGELO: *(getting angry)* Very funny, Antipholus. The money... now.

ANTIPHOLUS E: There was no chain and you're not getting any money.

ANGELO: Really?

MERCHANT: I have an idea. *(yells offstage)* OFFICER!

(OFFICER enters)

OFFICER: You called, sir?

ANGELO: Yes. This man refuses to pay me. Arrest him at my suit.

OFFICER: I charge you in the Duke's name.

ANTIPHOLUS E: This is ridiculous!

(DROMIO S enters)

DROMIO S: Sir, ummm... you've been arrested.

ANTIPHOLUS E: Really?! I didn't notice!

DROMIO S: By the way, I have secured passage on a ship!

ANTIPHOLUS E: What?! Man, you have been acting really weird lately! I'm tired of your antics. I asked for donuts, NOT A SHIP!

DROMIO S: Donuts?

ANTIPHOLUS E: Forget the donuts! Go to my wife, get money, so I can give thee bail!

DROMIO S: Money. Bail. Right! And... what about the ship?

ANTIPHOLUS E: Forget the ship! Forget the donuts! Man, you are dense!

DROMIO S: No ship! No donuts!

ANTIPHOLUS E: GO!!!

(ALL exit; moments later ADRIANA and LUCIANA enter)

LUCIANA: Adriana, you need to know this! Your husband told me he loved me! He is deranged! No... posses'd!

ADRIANA: Say what now?! What did you do?!

LUCIANA: Nothing! Except for being gorgeous, of course!

ADRIANA: Of course! That fool! Why do I love him so?!

(enter DROMIO S)

DROMIO S: Hello again!

ADRIANA: Where is thy master, Dromio?

DROMIO S: Ummm... your husband's been arrested and needs money.

ADRIANA: What, is he arrested?

DROMIO S: Uh, yeah, that's what I just said.

ADRIANA: What is going on with that fool?!

LUCIANA: Told you, deranged AND possess'd!

ADRIANA: Go, Dromio; there's the money. Keep my fool out of jail!

DROMIO S: Yes, ma'am!

(ALL exit)

(ANTIPHOLUS S enters)

ANTIPHOLUS S: *(to audience)* The people in this town are soooo nice! Totally weird, but nice. The weird thing? They all know my name. Strange, right?

(enter DROMIO S breathing heavy)

DROMIO S: Sir! Your money!

ANTIPHOLUS S: What money?! I didn't ask for any money.

DROMIO S: You know, bail for jail? You've been arrested...

ANTIPHOLUS S: Jail?! Arrested?! Man, you are going insane, too. What about the ships? Did you find us a ship to leave on?

DROMIO S: Ship?! You told me to forget about the ship. AND the donuts!

ANTIPHOLUS S: Donuts? I told you what?! This place is surely possessed! We need to leave soon!

(ALL exit)

ACT 4 SCENE 4

(enter ANTIPHOLUS E and DROMIO E)

DROMIO E: Here are the donuts you asked for, sir!

ANTIPHOLUS E: *(angry)* Donuts?! I don't need donuts; I need money to stay out of jail! But, I do like donuts. Give me those.

DROMIO E: Jail? Why are you going to jail?

ANTIPHOLUS E: Why, I oughta...

(ANTIPHOLUS E throws donut at DROMIO E, then chases around stage, stops abruptly when PINCH, ADRIANA, LUCIANA, and TOWNSFOLK enter)

ADRIANA: Dr. Pinch, I need you to take my husband, and his wacky servant, and get rid of the demons within them!

PINCH, DROMIO E, & ANTIPHOLUS E: DEMONS?!

ANTIPHOLUS E: Woah, wifey-poo, I ain't got no demons!

DROMIO E: And I'm not wacky!

ADRIANA: Quiet!!!

ANTIPHOLUS E: *(aside to DROMIO)* You are kind of wacky.

PINCH: Listen, lady, I'm only doing this sorcery gig as a side business because they don't pay me enough as a schoolteacher.

ADRIANA: Wait, but you're a doctor?

PINCH: Yes, but a doctor of history. So...

ADRIANA: Ohhhh... so... schoolteacher, I get it. Well, I don't care. Just do it!

PINCH: Okay, okay... pushy, pushy. But if they go crazy, I'm out of here!

ADRIANA: Fine, just get them!

PINCH: Team, round them up! Both man and master is possess'd!

(chaos ensues; ANTIPHOLUS E and DROMIO E are tied up by TOWNSFOLK)

PINCH: Take them to the basement! The fiend is strong within them.

(ANTIPHOLUS E and DROMIO E are led offstage; PINCH follows)

ANTIPHOLUS E: *(exiting)* I am not mad I tell you!!! NOT MAD!

DROMIO E: And I'm not wacky!

LUCIANA: Oh, he is definitely mad!

ADRIANA: Whew! I'm finally glad they're gone.

(ANTIPHOLUS S and DROMIO S enter opposite)

ANTIPHOLUS S: Hello!

ADRIANA: For thy mercy! They are loose again.

LUCIANA: Let's get out of here!

(ADRIANA and LUCIANA exit screaming)

DROMIO S: Huh. Must have been something you said.

ANTIPHOLUS S: This place is insane! Fetch our stuff and let's leave tonight.

DROMIO S: Agreed!

(ALL exit)

ACT 5 SCENE 1

(enter ANGELO)

ANGELO: *(to audience)* Antipholus has a great reputation, is highly beloved, and wealthy! But, I need that money. Here he comes now. And he's wearing the chain about his neck!

(enter ANTIPHOLUS S and DROMIO S)

ANTIPHOLUS S: Dromio, we need to get out of here soon!

ANGELO: YOU! I demand payment.

DROMIO S: Very soon. This town is absolutely cuckoo!

ANGELO: I do defy thee for a villain.

ANTIPHOLUS S: How dare you call me a villain!

(ALL draw swords and prepare to fight; pause, then ADRIANA, LUCIANA, and TOWNSFOLK enter)

DROMIO S: The crazy lady approaches.

LUCIANA: There he is!

ADRIANA: He is mad! Take his sword away!

DROMIO S: Run, master, run! Into the priory!

(ANTIPHOLUS S and DROMIO S exit)

ADRIANA: Get them!

(TOWNSFOLK follow but can't "enter")

TOWNSFOLK: It is locked!

(enter ABBESS)

ABBESS: Hello. May I help you?

ADRIANA: Yes! My loony husband is in there. I demand you let him out!

ABBESS: He is only loony because you are a jealous, and loud, woman.

ADRIANA: WHAT!?! I AM NOT... jealous.

ABBESS: I will cure what ails him. Now leave. Not a creature enters in my house. Good day. *(exits)*

ADRIANA: Who does she think she is?!

LUCIANA: You ARE kind of loud sometimes...

ADRIANA: I AM NOT! Achemm... I am not. I have a firm voice.

LUCIANA: Okay...

(enter DUKE and EGEON; all kneel)

DUKE: Egeon, the time has come. *(to audience)* I need to proclaim it publicly. If any friend shall pay the sum for him, he shall not die. *(silence)* Very well. Tough luck, Egeon.

EGEON: Yes, luck. I need just a bit more of it.

ADRIANA: Justice, most sacred duke, against the abbess!

DUKE: I'm sorry, what? Can't you see I'm about to behead someone?

EGEON: No, no. Go on about your business. I'm good.

DUKE: Very well.

ADRIANA: The abbess is holding my husband captive! Demand she lets him go!

DUKE: Your husband has served me well over the years. I shall help. *(approaches priory)*

(TOWNSFOLK looks and points offstage)

TOWNSFOLK: O mistress, mistress, your husband and his man are both broke loose.

ADRIANA: Peace, fool! Thy master and his man are here.

TOWNSFOLK: Then who are they?!

(enter ANTIPHOLUS E and DROMIO E)

ALL: What?!!!

ADRIANA: Ay me, it is my husband! You see that, right?

LUCIANA: *(nodding confused)* Uh, huh.

ANTIPHOLUS E: This has been the strangest day, ever!

DROMIO E: Yes, it has!

EGEON: *(to audience)* What luck! Unless the fear of death doth make me dote, I see my son Antipholus and Dromio.

ADRIANA: *(to ANTIPHOLUS E)* Who are you?!

ANTIPHOLUS E: I am your husband, dear woman!

ADRIANA: Are not!

ANTIPHOLUS E: Are too!

ADRIANA: Nope! My husband is in there! *(points offstage)* I think.

DUKE: What is going on here?!

ANTIPHOLUS E: This WOMAN has locked me out of my house. The goldsmith accused me of stealing a chain. The merchant had me arrested. And then Pinch, a hungry lean-faced villain, cries out, I was possess'd! Bounded me and tossed me into the basement!

DROMIO E: Me too!

ADRIANA: Clearly you ARE possess'd, because my husband is in there!

DUKE: Stop! You saw'st him enter the abbey here?

LUCIANA & ADRIANA: Yes!

DUKE: *(to TOWNSFOLK)* You! Go in and fetch the abbess.

(TOWNSFOLK exits; EGEON hugs ANTIPHOLUS E, who goes stiff, and pries off hug)

ANTIPHOLUS E: What is this? Who is this old man?

EGEON: Sir, are you call'd Antipholus? And your bondman, Dromio?

ANTIPHOLUS E: Maybe...

EGEON: Then you know me well. I am your father.

ALL: What?!!!

ANTIPHOLUS E: I never saw my father in my life.

DROMIO E: Truth!

EGEON: It's only been seven years since Syracuse. Surely you remember me?

ANTIPHOLUS E: Strange, old man, I've never been to Syracuse.

(enter TOWNSFOLK, ABBESS, ANTIPHOLUS S, and DROMIO S)

ABBESS: Most mighty duke, behold a man much wrong'd.

ADRIANA: I see two husbands, or mine eyes deceive me.

ANTIPHOLUS S: Dad?!

EGEON: Son! *(they embrace)*

DROMIO S: Old master! *(hugs them both)* Who hath bound him here?

ABBESS: Whoever bound him, I will loose his bonds. For, he has just gained a wife.

ALL: WHAT?!!!

ABBESS: Tis true! My name is Emilia, and we once had two fair sons.

EGEON: Dear Emilia! *(they hug)* But what happened to our son?

ABBESS: Antipholus and his servant, Dromio, were forced from me when we washed to shore. I had not seen them since, well... today.

ANTIPHOLUS S & E: Mom?!

ABBESS: Sons! *(all hug)*

ADRIANA: I've got a mother-in-law?

ANTIPHOLUS E: Mom, this is my wife, Adriana.

ABBESS: Bring it in, daughter! *(they hug)*

ANGELO: And the gold chain?

ANTIPHOLUS S: Oh, yes. This must be yours then. *(hands ANTIPHOLUS E chain)*

ANTIPHOLUS E: And this must be your money. *(pays ANGELO)*

ANGELO: Great!

ANTIPHOLUS E: These ducats pawn I for my father here.

DUKE: It shall not need; thy father hath his life.

ALL: Yay!

ABBESS: Great! It's been thirty-three years, time to party!

DUKE: With all my heart, I'll gossip at this feast.

ANTIPHOLUS S: Well, this is a great ending! *(grabs LUCIANA'S hand)* Now, let's get married!

LUCIANA: What? I'm sorry, you're cute and all, but... no.

ANTIPHOLUS S: Wait a minute! This is a Shakespeare comedy. EVERYONE gets married at the end of a Shakespeare comedy.

LUCIANA: Funny. I'm still gonna make you work for it. See ya! *(runs offstage)*

ANTIPHOLUS S: Feisty! I like her! *(sees ANTIPHOLUS E, claps his shoulder)* Embrace thy brother. *(they hug)*

ANTIPHOLUS E: Ready to party?

ANTIPHOLUS S: Absolutely!

(ALL exit except the DROMIOS)

DROMIO S: *(looking at DROMIO E)* Man, I am good-looking!

DROMIO E: Yes, you are!

DROMIO S: Let's go celebrate!

DROMIO E: Yes! Let's go hand in hand, not one before another.

(they link arms and exit)

THE END

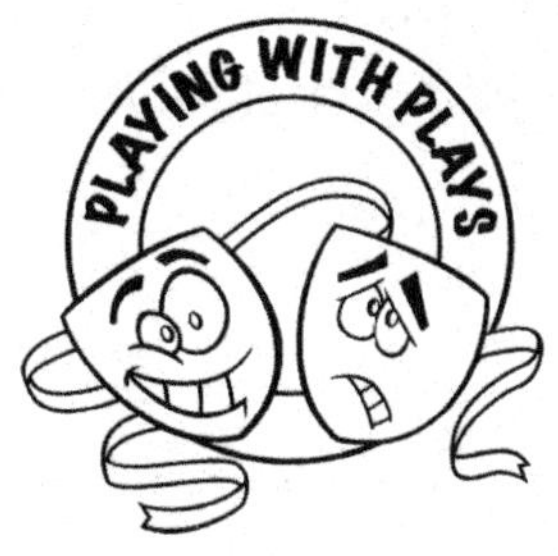

The 25-Minute or so Comedy of Errors
By William Shakespeare
Creatively modified by
Brendan P. Kelso
14 - 21+ Actors

CAST OF CHARACTERS:

[1]**DUKE:** Duke of Ephesus

[2]**EGEON:** father looking for his family

ANTIPHOLUS OF SYRACUSE: twin son

DROMIO OF SYRACUSE: another twin, and servant of Antipholus of Syracuse

ANTIPHOLUS OF EPHESUS: twin son

DROMIO OF EPHESUS: yes, another twin, and yes, servant of Antipholus of Ephesus

[3]**LADY ABBESS:** long lost mother of all!

ADRIANA: wife of Antipholus of Ephesus

LUCIANA: sister of Adriana

ANGELO: goldsmith, maker of nice bling

[4]**BALTHASAR:** a merchant with an actual name

[3]**LUCE:** Antipholus E's maid (offstage role)

[1]**INNKEEPER:** the keeper of inns

[4]**OFFICER:** keeper of the law

[2]**DR. PINCH:** daytime teacher/nighttime conjurer

[5]**FIRST MERCHANT:** a merchant with no name
SECOND MERCHANT: another merchant with no name
[5]**THIRD MERCHANT:** yep, another
[5]**MESSENGER:** delivers a message
TOWNSFOLK: a person from town
[4]**BAKER:** cooks yummy stuff

The same actors can play the following part:
[1]DUKE and INNKEEPER
[2]EGEON and DR. PINCH
[3]LADY ABESS and LUCE
[4]BALTHASAR, OFFICER, and BAKER
[5]FIRST MERCHANT, THIRD MERCHANT, and MESSENGER
TOWNSFOLK can be extras and randomly inserted throughout play

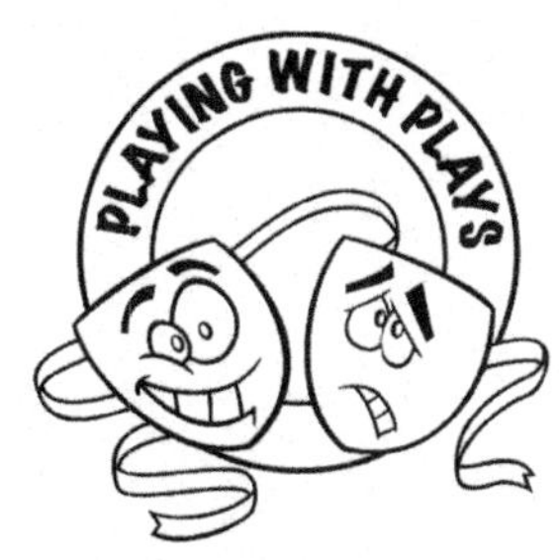

ACT 1 SCENE 1

(DUKE and EGEON enter)

DUKE: You seem like a decent fellow, Egeon. I hate to kill you.

EGEON: You seem like a decent fellow, Duke. I hate to die.

DUKE: Tell me, before I run you through, how did you come to be in our fair city of Ephesus?

EGEON: I came looking for my lost family.

DUKE: So you lost your family and now you're going to lose your life? Rough day.

EGEON: Yes, we had twin boys, but my wife and the boys were separated at sea.

DUKE: Twins, huh?

EGEON: Yes, and THEY had twin servants, who were also separated.

DUKE: Twin servants, for twin boys? Interesting! Confusing, but interesting!

EGEON: It's way more complicated than that, you know, Shakespeare.

DUKE: *(DUKE nods)* Ah, Shakespeare. Keeping people confused since 1590!

EGEON: Exactly. But, to keep it simple, I never found my wife, my other son, or his servant, and now I'm searching the world for them!

DUKE: Touching story. I'll tell you what. Instead of killing you today, I'll kill you tomorrow. A passed sentence may not be recall'd, but I will grant you one day!

EGEON: That is so kind of you!

DUKE: I try. Go! Try to find your family. I know you've failed these past thirty-three years, but something tells me this next twenty-four hours will be different! Go!

EGEON: *(running off)* Thank you! Thank you!!!

DUKE: *(to audience)* I'm such a good duke.

(DUKE exits)

(ANTIPHOLUS S, DROMIO S, enter looking like tourists; FIRST MERCHANT enters opposite)

ANTIPHOLUS S: Excuse me, sir, what is the name of this city?

FIRST MERCHANT: Ephesus. Where are you from?

ANTIPHOLUS S: Syracuse.

FIRST MERCHANT: *(gasps)* Do you not know the statute of the town?

ANTIPHOLUS S: A statute? What law?

FIRST MERCHANT: Anyone from Syracuse has to pay 1,000 gold marks or be executed!

ANTIPHOLUS S: What?!?!

FIRST MERCHANT: Yes, some old man was to be executed this morning by the Duke, for this very same thing!

ANTIPHOLUS S: But I'm just here to look for my mom and long-lost brother.

FIRST MERCHANT: That's nice. But they'll kill ya anyway!!! See ya!

(FIRST MERCHANT exits)

ANTIPHOLUS S: Dromio!!!

DROMIO S: Yes, master Antipholus?

ANTIPHOLUS S: Quick, we can't look like travelers! Take our gear and my money to the Centaur, and get us a room.

DROMIO S: Very well, sir! Center room! But what hotel? *(overloaded with gear, fun chaos ensues as he leaves the stage)*

ANTIPHOLUS S: I just told you. The Centaur.

DROMIO S: Riiiight... Center room.

ANTIPHOLUS S: Noooo. CENTAUR HOTEL. *(acts like horse)*

DROMIO S: Ohhhhh... now that makes more sense.

ANTIPHOLUS S: Now go! *(DROMIO S exits; to audience)* Dromio is crazy. They sure don't make servants like they used to!

(DROMIO E enters opposite)

DROMIO E: There you are, master!

ANTIPHOLUS S: Wow, Dromio, thou art return'd so soon? Didn't you just... *(points opposite)* never mind.

DROMIO E: *(confused)* Return'd so soon? Rather approached too late.

ANTIPHOLUS S: Huh?

DROMIO E: Huh?

ANTIPHOLUS S: *(to audience)* See, my servant is crazy.

DROMIO E: Ummm, your wife sent me. Dinner is ready, and she wants you home now!

ANTIPHOLUS S: What in the world are you talking about?

DROMIO E: Ummm... happy wife, happy life?

ANTIPHOLUS S: Which I agree with. But you were supposed to deliver my luggage, not get me a wife. Now quit being a fool. Where have you left the money?

DROMIO E: Money?

ANTIPHOLUS S: Yes! My thousand gold marks! My possessions! I'm about to get mad. Big and ugly mad! Tell me, where is my money?

DROMIO E: Possessions? You mean your wife, right?

ANTIPHOLUS S: *(to audience)* Crazy!!!

ADRIANA: *(backstage)* I am no one's possession!

DROMIO E: There's your love now!

ANTIPHOLUS S: What in the world...

DROMIO E: You really are strange right now, sir.

ANTIPHOLUS S: I'm strange? You're the one saying I'm married. And where have you bestow'd my money?!

DROMIO E: *(slowly starts stepping back)* You are married and there is no money.

ANTIPHOLUS S: WHAT!!!!

(DROMIO E runs offstage)

ANTIPHOLUS S: Dark-working sorcerers have changed his mind!!! This town is full of cozenage! Trickery abounds! *(runs off opposite)*

ACT 2 SCENE I

(enter ADRIANA and LUCIANA)

ADRIANA: Where is Antipholus? Neither my husband nor the slave return'd. Dinner is getting cold!

LUCIANA: Adriana, be patient sister, and wait for your husband. You need to be a good wife.

ADRIANA: I'm sorry, what? Luciana, are you wedded?

LUCIANA: Ah, no...

ADRIANA: That's right, you're not. I'm no homemaker! He does NOT control me. Bite your tongue till the day YOU have a husband!

LUCIANA: I'm just saying, this is the 1600s, women don't have any rights.

ADRIANA: Well, we'll just see about that!

(enter DROMIO E)

ADRIANA: Where is my husband!?

DROMIO E: Well, ma'am, he's acting REALLY weird and keeps saying, "No house, no wife... My gold! My gold!"

ADRIANA: *(grabs DROMIO'S ear)* Go back again and fetch him home.

DROMIO E: But he'll be mad! Please, send some other messenger!

ADRIANA: Back, Dromio, or I will break your head.

DROMIO E: I'll fetch thy master! *(exits)*

ADRIANA: And don't return without him!

DROMIO E: *(offstage)* Yes ma'am!

ADRIANA: *(to LUCIANA)* Servants these days.

(ALL exit)

ACT 2 SCENE 2

(enter ANTIPHOLUS S and INNKEEPER)

ANTIPHOLUS S: *(to audience)* Let's see what that bold-faced liar actually did with my money! *(to INNKEEPER)* Hello innkeeper, I was wondering if my luggage was dropped off earlier?

INNKEEPER: Yes! And a thousand gold marks as well. It's all stored in the back.

ANTIPHOLUS S: Really? Okay... thanks.

(INNKEEPER exits)

ANTIPHOLUS S: Well, that is strange.

(enter DROMIO S)

ANTIPHOLUS S: YOU!

DROMIO S: ME!

ANTIPHOLUS S: Don't 'me', me!

DROMIO S: Huh? Why would I 'you', you?

ANTIPHOLUS S: Why did you lie to me?

DROMIO S: Huh?

ANTIPHOLUS S: All this nonsense about a mistress and a dinner!

DROMIO S: Huh?

ANTIPHOLUS S: You did just what I asked!

DROMIO S: Right.

ANTIPHOLUS S: Right!

DROMIO S: Soooo...

ANTIPHOLUS S: Soooo... I'm confused. Know any good jokes?

DROMIO S: Of course! Why did the chicken cross the playground?

ANTIPHOLUS S: Ummm, dunno.

DROMIO S: To get to the other SLIDE!

(they laugh)

DROMIO S: Okay, okay... what do you call a fake noodle?

ANTIPHOLUS S: I don't know.

DROMIO S: Impasta!!!

(they laugh; enter ADRIANA and LUCIANA, they stare for a moment, then ADRIANA coughs expectantly)

ADRIANA: Ay, Ay, Antipholus, wipe that silly smirk off your face.

ANTIPHOLUS S: I'm sorry, I know you not.

ADRIANA: Excuse me?

LUCIANA: Fie, brother! How dare you talk to your wife that way?

ADRIANA: I can handle this, Luciana. How dare you talk to your wife that way?!

LUCIANA: Yeah!

ANTIPHOLUS S: More of this wife stuff? What is going on here?

LUCIANA: She sent for you by Dromio home to dinner.

ANTIPHOLUS S: By Dromio?

DROMIO S: What?! By me?

ADRIANA & LUCIANA: YES!

DROMIO S: Who are these chicks?

ADRIANA: Chicks?

DROMIO S: Sorry. Babes.

LUCIANA: Babes?!

DROMIO S: I think the lady doth protest too much!

(MEN laugh)

ADRIANA: That's it! Come back home, now!

(grabs their ears and drags them offstage; ALL exit, then return still dragging them by their ears; she lets go)

ANTIPHOLUS S: Okay, okay... I'll be your husband, sheesh.

ADRIANA: That's more like it.

LUCIANA: Yeah! What she said.

ADRIANA: Dromio, guard this door. You, *(pointing at ANTIPHOLUS S)* let's go eat!

ANTIPHOLUS S: *(to DROMIO)* Well, at least I get a meal out of it.

(ALL exit)

(ANTIPHOLUS E, DROMIO E, BALTHASAR, and ANGELO enter)

ANTIPHOLUS E: Angelo, Balthasar, I'll have my wife make us a great meal. Dromio, open the gates for us.

DROMIO E: Yes, master Antipholus.

BALTHASAR: I'm looking forward to this great meal, Antipholus.

ANGELO: Your wife's cooking is the best!

ANTIPHOLUS E: It is. It is. What is taking so long, Dromio?

DROMIO E: It is locked.

ANTIPHOLUS E: Well, knock on it, you fool!

(DROMIO "knocks" on door)

DROMIO S: *(offstage)* Yes?

DROMIO E: Let us in!

DROMIO S: No!

DROMIO E: Sir, apparently, they won't let us in.

ANTIPHOLUS E: What?! *("knocks")*

DROMIO S: Yes?

ANTIPHOLUS E: I demand you to let us in!

DROMIO S: No!

ANTIPHOLUS E: WHAT?! I am the master of this house. Let us in!

DROMIO S: Ummm... No?

ANTIPHOLUS E: WHAT?! LET US IN NOWWWWWWW!!!

LUCE: *(offstage)* What is all this ruckus?

ANTIPHOLUS E: Luce, it's Antipholus, let me in!

LUCE: Sorry, the master says no!

ANTIPHOLUS E: I AM the master!!!

LUCE: Riiiiight.

DROMIO E: Keep knocking, master!

LUCE: You can knock till it ache. Goodbye!

ANTIPHOLUS E: Let's break down the door!

BALTHASAR: Perhaps we should not.

ANTIPHOLUS E: What?!

BALTHASAR: Well, maybe your wife has a reason for keeping you out?

ANTIPHOLUS E: A reason?

ANGELO: Yes! Maybe she's planning a surprise party!

ANTIPHOLUS E: My birthday is not for another six months!

ANGELO: She's a planner?

ANTIPHOLUS E: Arghh! Let's just go into town. I'll clear this up tomorrow.

BALTHASAR: Sounds good.

ANTIPHOLUS E: By the way, Angelo, can you make me a gold chain? I need something to make me happy.

ANGELO: You got it! I'll bring it by tomorrow.

ANTIPHOLUS E: Great! To the town!

(ALL exit)

ACT 3 SCENE 2

(enter ANTIPHOLUS S and LUCIANA a moment later yelling)

LUCIANA: I can't believe you are treating my sister, YOUR WIFE, with such disrespect!

ANTIPHOLUS S: Sweet mistress, in my defense...

LUCIANA: Don't sweet mistress me! Enough of the insolence! You have been childish, rude, arrogant, and vain.

ANTIPHOLUS S: Wow. You're feisty!

LUCIANA: Excuse me?!

ANTIPHOLUS S: *(grabs his heart)* Wait! What's that feeling? Oh, no! I think I just fell in love with you!

LUCIANA: What?! Are you mad?! You can't say that!!!

ANTIPHOLUS S: It's Shakespeare, sure I can!

LUCIANA: Arghhhh!!!! Adriana!!! Your husband just told me he loves me! *(exits yelling)*

ANTIPHOLUS S: Oh, no! No, no, nooo... oh well. *(to audience)* I like her!

(enter DROMIO S)

DROMIO S: Hey boss! Get this: Luce, the lady that runs the kitchen, thinks I'm her husband!

ANTIPHOLUS S: What? What is it with all these women?

DROMIO S: Not sure. Don't you think it's really weird that she thinks I'm her husband and Adriana thinks you're her husband?

ANTIPHOLUS S: Totally! I mean, what are the odds of BOTH of them mistaking us for their spouses?

DROMIO S: Hold on. This is too coincidental.

ANTIPHOLUS S: Are you thinking what I'm thinking?

DROMIO S: I think so!

ANTIPHOLUS S: That we should get the heck out of this town because witches do inhabit here?

DROMIO S: Exactly!!!

ANTIPHOLUS S: Great, go down to the docks and book passage to leave tonight.

DROMIO S: I'm on it!

(DROMIO S exits)

ANTIPHOLUS S: *(to audience)* But, Luciana! Her beauty, and feistiness, make me never want to leave! Buuuut... on the other hand... witches. Oh! I have been enchanted!

(enter ANGELO)

ANGELO: Master Antipholus.

ANTIPHOLUS S: Ay, that's my name.

ANGELO: Here is the gold chain. I have made it for you. *(puts it on ANTIPHOLUS)*

ANTIPHOLUS S: Made it for me? I didn't request it.

ANGELO: That looks gooood! Payment? *(puts hand out)*

ANTIPHOLUS S: What? I don't want any necklace! And I don't have any money!

ANGELO: Just pay me later! Fare you well! *(exits)*

ANTIPHOLUS S: But I didn't order it! This town is bonkers. *(examines it; to audience)* Although, I do make it look good! Maybe I will keep it. *(exits)*

(ANGELO enters, SECOND MERCHANT enters opposite)

SECOND MERCHANT: Angelo! I'm glad to see you. I need the money you owe me.

ANGELO: Yeah... about that. Antipholus owes me that exact amount by five o'clock. Once I collect, I will pay you back!

SECOND MERCHANT: You better. I wouldn't want to "collect" some other way.

ANGELO: You and me both!

(enter ANTIPHOLUS E and DROMIO E)

DROMIO E: Sir, that was a chilly night. Are we going home today?

ANTIPHOLUS E: Yes, we will. In the meantime, go get me donuts. I like donuts.

DROMIO E: Donuts! Yes, sir! *(exits)*

(ANGELO coughs expectantly)

ANTIPHOLUS E: Angelo! Sorry about dinner last night.

ANGELO: That's okay. How about you give me the money you owe me for the gold chain I made you? I stand debted to this gentleman.

ANTIPHOLUS E: I'm sorry, what?

ANGELO: The gold chain. I gave it to you at your house. Just an hour ago. I need the money.

ANTIPHOLUS E: My house? Gave me a gold chain? Whatever are you talking about?

ANGELO: *(getting angry)* Very funny, Antipholus. The money... now.

ANTIPHOLUS E: There was no chain and you're not getting any money.

ANGELO: Really?

SECOND MERCHANT: I have an idea. *(yells offstage)* OFFICER!

(OFFICER enters)

OFFICER: You called, sir?

ANGELO: Yes. This man refuses to pay me. Arrest him at my suit.

OFFICER: I charge you in the Duke's name.

ANTIPHOLUS E: This is ridiculous!

(DROMIO S enters)

DROMIO S: Sir, ummm... you've been arrested.

ANTIPHOLUS E: Really?! I didn't notice!

DROMIO S: By the way, I have secured passage on a ship!

ANTIPHOLUS E: What?! Man, you have been acting really weird lately! I'm tired of your antics. I asked for donuts, NOT A SHIP!

DROMIO S: Donuts?

ANTIPHOLUS E: Forget the donuts! Go to my wife, get money, so I can give thee bail!

DROMIO S: Money. Bail. Right! And... what about the ship?

ANTIPHOLUS E: Forget the ship! Forget the donuts! Man, you are dense!

DROMIO S: No ship! No donuts!

ANTIPHOLUS E: GO!!!

(ALL exit; moments later ADRIANA and LUCIANA enter)

LUCIANA: Adriana, you need to know this! Your husband told me he loved me! He is deranged! No... posses'd!

ADRIANA: Say what now?! What did you do?!

LUCIANA: Nothing! Except for being gorgeous, of course!

ADRIANA: Of course! That fool! Why do I love him so?!

(enter DROMIO S)

DROMIO S: Hello again!

ADRIANA: Where is thy master, Dromio?

DROMIO S: Ummm... your husband's been arrested and needs money.

ADRIANA: What, is he arrested?

DROMIO S: Uh, yeah, that's what I just said.

ADRIANA: What is going on with that fool?!

LUCIANA: Told you, deranged AND possess'd!

ADRIANA: Go, Dromio; there's the money. Keep my fool out of jail!

DROMIO S: Yes, ma'am!

(ALL exit)

(ANTIPHOLUS S enters opposite THIRD MERCHANT)

THIRD MERCHANT: Hello, Antipholus!

ANTIPHOLUS S: Hello?

THIRD MERCHANT: Good day, isn't it?

ANTIPHOLUS S: Yes. Yes, it is.

(THIRD MERCHANT exits; enter BAKER)

BAKER: Antipholus, did you enjoy the cake I made you the other day?!

ANTIPHOLUS S: Ummm, yes, it was delicious?

BAKER: Great! Enjoy the day! *(exits)*

ANTIPHOLUS S: *(to audience)* The people in this town are soooo nice! Totally weird, but nice. The weird thing? They all know my name. Strange, right?

(enter DROMIO S breathing heavy)

DROMIO S: Sir! Your money!

ANTIPHOLUS S: What money?! I didn't ask for any money.

DROMIO S: You know, bail for jail? You've been arrested...

ANTIPHOLUS S: Jail?! Arrested?! Man, you are going insane, too. What about the ships? Did you find us a ship to leave on?

DROMIO S: Ship?! You told me to forget about the ship. AND the donuts!

ANTIPHOLUS S: Donuts? I told you what?! This place is surely possessed! We need to leave soon!

(ALL exit)

ACT 4 SCENE 4

(enter ANTIPHOLUS E and DROMIO E)

DROMIO E: Here are the donuts you asked for, sir!

ANTIPHOLUS E: *(angry)* Donuts?! I don't need donuts; I need money to stay out of jail! But, I do like donuts. Give me those.

DROMIO E: Jail? Why are you going to jail?

ANTIPHOLUS E: Why, I oughta...

(ANTIPHOLUS E throws donut at DROMIO E, then chases around stage, stops abruptly when PINCH, ADRIANA, LUCIANA, and TOWNSFOLK enter)

ADRIANA: Dr. Pinch, I need you to take my husband, and his wacky servant, and get rid of the demons within them!

PINCH, DROMIO E, & ANTIPHOLUS E: DEMONS?!

ANTIPHOLUS E: Woah, wifey-poo, I ain't got no demons!

DROMIO E: And I'm not wacky!

ADRIANA: Quiet!!!

ANTIPHOLUS E: *(aside to DROMIO)* You are kind of wacky.

PINCH: Listen, lady, I'm only doing this sorcery gig as a side business because they don't pay me enough as a schoolteacher.

ADRIANA: Wait, but you're a doctor?

PINCH: Yes, but a doctor of history. So...

ADRIANA: Ohhhh... so... schoolteacher, I get it. Well, I don't care. Just do it!

PINCH: Okay, okay... pushy, pushy. But if they go crazy, I'm out of here!

ADRIANA: Fine, just get them!

PINCH: Team, round them up! Both man and master is possess'd!

(chaos ensues; ANTIPHOLUS E and DROMIO E are tied up)

PINCH: Take them to the basement! The fiend is strong within them.

(ANTIPHOLUS E and DROMIO E are led offstage; PINCH follows)

ANTIPHOLUS E: *(exiting)* I am not mad I tell you!!! NOT MAD!

DROMIO E: And I'm not wacky!

LUCIANA: Oh, he is definitely mad!

ADRIANA: Whew! I'm finally glad they're gone.

(ANTIPHOLUS S and DROMIO S enter opposite)

ANTIPHOLUS S: Hello!

ADRIANA: For thy mercy! They are loose again.

LUCIANA: Let's get out of here!

(ADRIANA and LUCIANA exit screaming)

DROMIO S: Huh. Must have been something you said.

ANTIPHOLUS S: This place is insane! Fetch our stuff and let's leave tonight.

DROMIO S: Agreed!

(ALL exit)

ACT 5 SCENE 1

(enter SECOND MERCHANT and ANGELO)

SECOND MERCHANT: I need that money, Angelo, or you'll be arrested next!

ANGELO: You'll get paid! Antipholus has a great reputation, is highly beloved, and wealthy! Here he comes now. And he's wearing the chain about his neck!

(enter ANTIPHOLUS S and DROMIO S)

ANTIPHOLUS S: Dromio, we need to get out of here soon!

ANGELO: YOU! I demand payment.

DROMIO S: Very soon. This town is absolutely cuckoo!

SECOND MERCHANT: I do defy thee for a villain.

ANTIPHOLUS S: How dare you call me a villain!

(ALL draw swords and prepare to fight; pause, then ADRIANA, LUCIANA, and TOWNSFOLK enter)

DROMIO S: The crazy lady approaches.

LUCIANA: There he is!

ADRIANA: He is mad! Take his sword away!

DROMIO S: Run, master, run! Into the priory!

(ANTIPHOLUS S and DROMIO S exit)

ADRIANA: Get them!

(TOWNSFOLK follow but can't "enter")

TOWNSFOLK: It is locked!

(enter ABBESS)

ABBESS: Hello. May I help you?

ADRIANA: Yes! My loony husband is in there. I demand you let him out!

ABBESS: He is only loony because you are a jealous, and loud, woman.

ADRIANA: WHAT!?! I AM NOT... jealous.

ABBESS: I will cure what ails him. Now leave. Not a creature enters in my house. Good day. *(exits)*

ADRIANA: Who does she think she is?!

LUCIANA: You ARE kind of loud sometimes...

ADRIANA: I AM NOT! Achemm... I am not. I have a firm voice.

LUCIANA: Okay...

(enter DUKE and EGEON; all kneel)

DUKE: Egeon, the time has come. *(to audience)* I need to proclaim it publicly. If any friend shall pay the sum for him, he shall not die. *(silence)* Very well. Tough luck, Egeon.

EGEON: Yes, luck. I need just a bit more of it.

ADRIANA: Justice, most sacred duke, against the abbess!

DUKE: I'm sorry, what? Can't you see I'm about to behead someone?

EGEON: No, no. Go on about your business. I'm good.

DUKE: Very well.

ADRIANA: The abbess is holding my husband captive! Demand she lets him go!

DUKE: Your husband has served me well over the years. I shall help. *(approaches priory)*

(enter MESSENGER opposite to ADRIANA)

MESSENGER: O mistress, mistress, your husband and his man are both broke loose.

ADRIANA: Peace, fool! Thy master and his man are here.

MESSENGER: Then who are they?!

(enter ANTIPHOLUS E and DROMIO E)

ALL: What?!!!

ADRIANA: Ay me, it is my husband! You see that, right?

LUCIANA: *(nodding confused)* Uh, huh.

ANTIPHOLUS E: This has been the strangest day, ever!

DROMIO E: Yes, it has!

EGEON: *(to audience)* What luck! Unless the fear of death doth make me dote, I see my son Antipholus and Dromio.

ADRIANA: *(to ANTIPHOLUS E)* Who are you?!

ANTIPHOLUS E: I am your husband, dear woman!

ADRIANA: Are not!

ANTIPHOLUS E: Are too!

ADRIANA: Nope! My husband is in there! *(points offstage)* I think.

DUKE: What is going on here?!

ANTIPHOLUS E: This WOMAN has locked me out of my house. The goldsmith accused me of stealing a chain. The merchant had me arrested. And then Pinch, a hungry lean-faced villain, cries out, I was possess'd! Bounded me and tossed me into the basement!

DROMIO E: Me too!

ADRIANA: Clearly you ARE possess'd, because my husband is in there!

DUKE: Stop! You saw'st him enter the abbey here?

LUCIANA & ADRIANA: Yes!

DUKE: Messenger, go in and fetch the abbess.

(MESSENGER exits; EGEON hugs ANTIPHOLUS E, who goes stiff, and pries off hug)

ANTIPHOLUS E: What is this? Who is this old man?

EGEON: Sir, are you call'd Antipholus? And your bondman, Dromio?

ANTIPHOLUS E: Maybe...

EGEON: Then you know me well. I am your father.

ALL: What?!!!

ANTIPHOLUS E: I never saw my father in my life.

DROMIO E: Truth!

EGEON: It's only been seven years since Syracuse. Surely you remember me?

ANTIPHOLUS E: Strange, old man, I've never been to Syracuse.

(enter MESSENGER, ABBESS, ANTIPHOLUS S, and DROMIO S)

ABBESS: Most mighty duke, behold a man much wrong'd.

ADRIANA: I see two husbands, or mine eyes deceive me.

ANTIPHOLUS S: Dad?!

EGEON: Son! *(they embrace)*

DROMIO S: Old master! *(hugs them both)* Who hath bound him here?

ABBESS: Whoever bound him, I will loose his bonds. For, he has just gained a wife.

ALL: WHAT?!!!

ABBESS: Tis true! My name is Emilia, and we once had two fair sons.

EGEON: Dear Emilia! *(they hug)* But what happened to our son?

ABBESS: Antipholus and his servant, Dromio, were forced from me when we washed to shore. I had not seen them since, well... today.

ANTIPHOLUS S & E: Mom?!

ABBESS: Sons! *(all hug)*

ADRIANA: I've got a mother-in-law?

ANTIPHOLUS E: Mom, this is my wife, Adriana.

ABBESS: Bring it in, daughter! *(they hug)*

ANGELO: And the gold chain?

ANTIPHOLUS S: Oh, yes. This must be yours then. *(hands ANTIPHOLUS E chain)*

ANTIPHOLUS E: And this must be your money. *(pays ANGELO)*

ANGELO: Great!

(SECOND MERCHANT snatches money from ANGELO)

SECOND MERCHANT: And thank you! *(exits)*

ANTIPHOLUS E: These ducats pawn I for my father here.

DUKE: It shall not need; thy father hath his life.

ALL: Yay!

ABBESS: Great! It's been thirty-three years, time to party!

DUKE: With all my heart, I'll gossip at this feast.

ANTIPHOLUS S: Well, this is a great ending! *(grabs LUCIANA'S hand)* Now, let's get married!

LUCIANA: What? I'm sorry, you're cute and all, but... no.

ANTIPHOLUS S: Wait a minute! This is a Shakespeare comedy. EVERYONE gets married at the end of a Shakespeare comedy.

LUCIANA: Funny. I'm still gonna make you work for it. See ya! *(runs offstage)*

ANTIPHOLUS S: Feisty! I like her! *(sees ANTIPHOLUS E, claps his shoulder)* Embrace thy brother. *(they hug)*

ANTIPHOLUS E: Ready to party?

ANTIPHOLUS S: Absolutely!

(ALL exit except the DROMIOS)

DROMIO S: *(looking at DROMIO E)* Man, I am good-looking!

DROMIO E: Yes, you are!

DROMIO S: Let's go celebrate!

DROMIO E: Yes! Let's go hand in hand, not one before another.

(they link arms and exit)

THE END

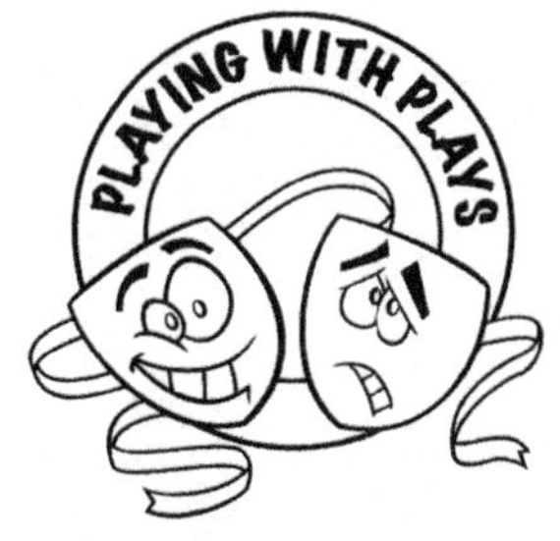

Special Thanks

And my shout outs to the educators who, with help of their kids, beta read this project and laughed along side of me!

David Ello, Laura Ah Mow, Lizette Winter, Jean Schubert, Christina Robart, Isidro Rodriguez, Bridget Adams, Lisa Miller, and Kevin Bell!

Thank you for helping me make this the best it can be!

Break some legs!

-Brendan

Sneak Peeks at other
Playing With Plays books:

The Tempest for Kids

PROSPERO: Hast thou, spirit, performed to point the tempest that I bade thee?

ARIEL: What? Was that English?

PROSPERO: *(Frustrated)* Did you make the storm hit the ship?

ARIEL: Why didn't you say that in the first place? Oh yeah! I rocked that ship! They didn't know what hit them.

PROSPERO: Why, that's my spirit! But are they, Ariel, safe?

ARIEL: Not a hair perished.

PROSPERO: Woo-hoo! All right. We've got more work to do.

ARIEL: Wait a minute. You're still going to free me, right, Master?

PROSPERO: Oh, I see. Is it sooooo terrible working for me? Huh? Remember when I saved you from that witch? Do you? Remember when that blue-eyed hag locked you up and left you for dead? Who saved you? Me, that's who!

ARIEL: I thank thee, master.

PROSPERO: I will free you in two days, okay? Sheesh. Patience is a virtue, or haven't you heard. Right. Where was I? Oh yeah... I need you to disguise yourself like a sea nymph and then... *(PROSPERO whispers something in ARIEL'S ear)* Got it?

ARIEL: Got it. *(ARIEL exits)*

PROSPERO: *(to MIRANDA)* Awake, dear heart, awake!

(MIRANDA yawns loudly)

PROSPERO: Shake it off. Come on. We'll visit Caliban, my slave.

MIRANDA: The witch's son? You mean the MONSTER! He's creepy and stinky!!!

PROSPERO: Mysterious and sneaky,

MIRANDA: Altogether freaky,

MIRANDA & PROSPERO: He's Caliban the slave!!! *(snap, snap!)*

PROSPERO: *(Calls offstage)* What, ho! Slave! Caliban!

(enter CALIBAN)

CALIBAN: Oh, look it's the island stealers! This is my home! My mother, the witch, left it to me and now you treat me like dirt.

MIRANDA: Oh boo-hoo! I used to feel sorry for you, I even taught you our language, but you tried to hurt me so now we have to lock you in that cave.

CALIBAN: I wish I had never learned your language!

PROSPERO: Go get us wood! If you don't, I'll rack thee with old cramps, and fill all thy bones with aches!

CALIBAN: *(to AUDIENCE)* He's so mean to me! But I have to do what he says. ANNOYING! *(exit CALIBAN)*

(enter FERDINAND led by "invisible" ARIEL)

ARIEL: *(Singing)* Who let the dogs out?! Woof, woof, woof!! *(Spookily)* The watchdogs bark; bow-wow, bow-wow!

FERDINAND: *(Dancing across stage)* Where should this music be? Where is it taking me! What's going on?

SCARECROW: We have to be careful in this forest.

TIN: W-w-w-why? W-w-w-what's here?

SCARECROW: Lions.

TIN: A-a-and?

SCARECROW: Tigers.

TIN: And?

SCARECROW: Bears!

DOROTHY: Oh, my! Lions, and tigers and...

(LION enters, roaring)

LION: Did you say lions?

DOROTHY: Well yes, but...

(roars again; DOROTHY bops LION)

LION: Ouch!

TOTO: Ruh Roh!

LION: What did you do that for?

DOROTHY: I was just about to break into a song.

LION: Oh, sorry. Please, go on.

DOROTHY: It's too late, you've ruined the moment.

LION: But, isn't this a musical?

DOROTHY: It was until you ruined it.

LION: Sorry.

DOROTHY: Don't apologize to me. Apologize to them... *(points to audience)*

LION: T-t-to them? But they're sc-c-cary!

TIN: Them? They're ordinary and dull looking.

SCARECROW: Especially that one. *(to LION)* What are you, a coward?

LION: Yes. Yes, I am. I'm a cowardly lion.

SCARECROW: Well, maybe the wizard can help you?

LION: The wizard?

TIN: That's a smart idea, Scarecrow! Yes, we are going to see the wizard for brains and a heart and something called Kansas!

DOROTHY: It's not a thing, it's my home!

LION: Do you think the wizard can give me courage?

DOROTHY: I don't see why not.

LION: Well then, do you mind if I join you? I'll roar very loudly to protect you!

SCARECROW: That would be wonderful!

TIN: Then we are off to see the wizard!

ALL: The wonderful Wizard of Oz!

Christmas Carol
for Kids

(enter GHOST PRESENT wearing a robe and holding a turkey leg and a goblet)

GHOST PRESENT: Wake up, Scrooge! I am the Ghost of Christmas Present. Look upon me!

SCROOGE: I'm looking. Not that impressed. But let's get on with it.

GHOST PRESENT: Touch my robe! *(SCROOGE touches GHOST PRESENT's robe. Pause. They look at each other)* Er...it must be broken. Guess we walk. Come on. *(they begin walking downstage)*

SCROOGE: Where are we going?

GHOST PRESENT: Your employee, Bob Cratchit's house. Oh look, here we are.

(enter BOB, MRS. CRATCHIT, MARTHA CRATCHIT, and TINY TIM, who has a crutch in one hand; they are all holding bowls)

BOB: *(to audience)* Hi, we're the Cratchit family. We are a REALLY happy family!

MRS. CRATCHIT: *(to audience)* Yes, but we're REALLY poor, too. Thanks to HIS boss! *(pointing at BOB)*

MARTHA: *(to audience)* Yeah, as you can see our bowls are empty. *(shows empty bowl)* We practically survive off air.

TINY TIM: *(to audience)* But we're happy!

MRS. CRATCHIT: *(to audience; overly sappy)* Because we have each other.

TINY TIM: And love!

SCROOGE: *(to GHOST PRESENT)* Seriously, are they for real?

GHOST PRESENT: Yep! Adorable, isn't it?

BOB: A merry Christmas to us all.

TINY TIM: God bless us every one!

SCROOGE: Spirit, tell me if Tiny Tim will live.

GHOST PRESENT: *(puts hands to head as if looking into the future)* Ooooo, not so good....I see a vacant seat in the poor chimney corner, and a crutch without an owner. If SOMEBODY doesn't change SOMETHING, the child will die.

SCROOGE: No, no! Say he will be spared.

GHOST PRESENT: Nope, can't do that, sorry. Unless SOMEONE decides to change...hint, hint.

BOB: A Christmas toast to my boss, Mr. Scrooge! The founder of the feast!

MRS. CRATCHIT: *(angrily)* Oh sure, Mr. Scrooge! If he were here I'd give him a piece of my mind to feast upon. What an odious, stingy, hard, unfeeling man!

BOB: Dear, it's Christmas day. He's not THAT bad. *(Pause)* He's just... THAT sad. *(BOB holds up his bowl)* Come on, kids, to Scrooge! He probably needs it more than us!

MARTHA & TINY TIM: *(holding up their bowls)* To Scrooge!

MRS. CRATCHIT: *(muttering)* Thanks for nothing.

BOB: That's not nice.

MARTHA: And we Cratchits are ALWAYS nice. Read

the book, Mom.

MRS. CRATCHIT: Sorry.

(the CRATCHIT FAMILY exits)

SCROOGE: She called me odious! Do I really smell that bad?

GHOST PRESENT: Odious doesn't mean you stink. Although in this case you do... According to the dictionary, odious means "unequivocally detestable." I mean, you are a toad sometimes Mr. Scrooge.

SCROOGE: Wow... that's kind of ... mean.

The Odyssey
for Kids

CREW 5: Look! Land!

YOUNG ODYSSEUS: Oh! I almost forgot; we can't stop here!

CREW: WHAT?!

YOUNG ODYSSEUS: It is the most dangerous place yet. Keep going!

CREW 5: They're just a bunch of cows, boss.

CREW 3: Maybe they are mutant cows that will eat us.

CREW 4: I'm tired of being eaten. I need to rest.

CREW 2: Me too!

CREW 6: I'm just tired!

CREW 1: Come on, sir. Let us stop.

YOUNG ODYSSEUS: Alright. Alright. But, you MUST promise not to harm a single cow.

CREW: Promise!

ODYSSEUS: *(to audience)* We came ashore and fell fast asleep. But, during the night, Zeus raised a great gale of wind, causing a hurricane.

CREW 1: Looks like we are stuck here.

YOUNG ODYSSEUS: We have lots of food on the ship. Remember, do NOT kill any cows!

CREW: Yes, sir! No cows!

ODYSSEUS: The hurricane blew for an entire month...

ALL: A MONTH!?!?

ODYSSEUS: We ran out of food. The days were long. I left my crew to take a nap. *(YOUNG ODYSSEUS exits)*

CREW 2: He naps at the strangest times.

CREW 3: I've never been this hungry in my life.

(COW enters)

COW: Moo.

CREW 4: Look! There's a nice, juicy hamburger. I-I-I mean cow.

COW: Moo?

CREW 5: Let's get it!

COW: Moo!!!

(CREW chases COW offstage, moo sounds from backstage, CREW enters licking their lips carrying "hamburger" supplies)

CREW 4: Now that hit the spot.

YOUNG ODYSSEUS: *(enters; sees hamburger paraphernalia)* Come on! I told you ONE thing. DO NOT eat the cows!

CREW 5: Sorry, boss. But it was only one.

CREW 4: And it was DELICIOUS!

CREW 1: Finally, the wind died down, and we set sail with full bellies!

(CREW rows)

CREW 2: As soon as we were away from the island, a black cloud formed over our ship.

CREW 3: It's Zeus!!!

ZEUS: *(enters)* Helios says you ate Bessie! My favorite bovine! *(stirs up a storm, ALL blow around stage)*

YOUNG ODYSSEUS: Told you not to eat the cows!

ODYSSEUS: *(to audience)* Zeus let fly his thunderbolts, the ship caught on fire, and the crew fell into the sea.

CREW 3: I guess this is it for us.

CREW 5: Nice knowing you!

CREW 4: That burger was worth it!!!

(CREW exits screaming, ZEUS exits happy)

Macbeth for Kids

ACT 2 SCENE 1

(DUNCAN runs on stage and dies with a dagger stuck in him, MACBETH drags his body off and then returns with the bloody dagger. LADY MACBETH enters)

LADY MACBETH: Did you do it?

MACBETH: *(clueless)* Do what?

LADY MACBETH: KILL HIM!

MACBETH: Oh yeah, all done. I have done the deed.

LADY MACBETH: *(pointing at the dagger)* What is that?

MACBETH: What?

LADY MACBETH: Why do you still have the bloody dagger with you?

MACBETH: Ummmmm, I don't know.

LADY MACBETH: Well go put it back!

MACBETH: NO! I'll go no more! I'm scared of the dark, and there is a dead body in there. I am afraid to think what I have done.

LADY MACBETH: Man you are a wimp, give me the dagger. *(LADY MACBETH takes the dagger, exits, and returns)*

LADY MACBETH: All done.

(there is a loud knock at the door)

LADY MACBETH: It's 2am! This really is not a good time for more visitors. *(goes to the door)* Who is it? *(opens door)*

MACDUFF: It is Macduff. I am here to see the king.

MACBETH: He is sleeping in there.

(MACDUFF exits while MACBETH and LADY MACBETH look at each other)

MACDUFF: *(offstage scream)* AGHHHHHHHHHHH – He's dead, he's dead!!! *(MACDUFF enters)*

MACBETH: Who?

MACDUFF: Who do you think? *(they both scream)*

BANQUO: *(BANQUO, MALCOLM, and DONALBAIN enter)* What happened, can't someone get a good night sleep around here?

MACDUFF: The king has been murdered.

MALCOLM & DONALBAIN: Aghhhhhhhh!!!!!!!!!

DONALBAIN: We must be next.

MALCOLM: Let's get out of here.

DONALBAIN: I'm heading to Ireland.

MALCOLM: I'm off to England. *(MALCOLM and DONALBAIN exit)*

MACDUFF: Well, since there is no one left to be King, why don't you do it Mac?

LADY MACBETH & MACBETH: Okay. *(LADY MACBETH, MACBETH and MACDUFF exit)*

BANQUO: *(to audience)* I fear, thou play'dst most foully for't. *(MACBETH returns)*

MACBETH: Bank, what are you thinking over there?

BANQUO: Oh, nothing. *(said with a big fake smile)* Gotta go! See ya! *(BANQUO exits)*

BRENDAN P. KELSO came to writing modified Shakespeare scripts when he was taking time off from work to be at home with his newly born son. "It just grew from there". Within months, he was being asked to offer classes in various locations and acting organizations along the Central Coast of California. Originally employed as an engineer, Brendan never thought about writing. However, his unique personality, humor, and love for engaging the kids with The Bard has led him to leave the engineering world and pursue writing as a new adventure in life! He has always believed, "the best way to learn is to have fun!" Brendan makes his home on the Central Coast of California and loves to spend time with his wife and kids.

CAST AUTOGRAPHS

Printed in Dunstable, United Kingdom